College Planning Strategies
I Wish Somebody Had Told Me:
The Ultimate Guide for Scholars and Parents

Dr. Christie Chamblis Murray

Outskirts Press, Inc.
http://www.outskirtspress.com

ISBN: 978-1-9772-0321-2

Library of Congress Control Number: 2018911269

Cover Photo and Design © 2018 Dr. Christie Chamblis Murray

Outskirts Press and the "OP" logo are trademarks belonging to Outskirts Press, Inc.

PRINTED IN THE UNITED STATES OF AMERICA

To my Special Ks...Kendall and Kameron.

ABOUT THE AUTHOR

Dr. Christie Chamblis Murray, born in Montgomery, Alabama, and educated in Chesapeake, Virginia is a graduate of Hampton University. She is a lifelong scholar and educator who has over 25 years of experience in engineering, business, strategic planning, leadership development, public safety, strategic communications, risk management, program management, professional speaking, and results-based facilitation. Dr. Murray wrote this book to share her personal educational and college planning experiences with others who are in pursuit of personal and academic excellence. She believes that knowledge is *POWER* and her intent is to close the youth educational opportunity gap by amplifying college planning awareness and helping others realize their college dreams. Dr. Murray's goal is to encourage middle and high school scholars to attend college and to believe that college is within their reach.

After meeting scholars and parents throughout her community in search of useful college planning and funding information, Dr. Murray knew there were others out there who might also benefit from these planning strategies. She also encountered others who appeared overwhelmed by the amount of information found on the Internet. This book will serve as a useful resource to individuals and families who are: (1) unclear on how to start and (2) unsure about how to finish the college planning process. May this book find itself in the hands of scholars and parents who need it the most!

Dr. Christie Chamblis Murray

Phone: (571) 310-1764

Email: author.christiemurray@investnothers.com

Website: https://www.investnothers.com/college-planning

TABLE OF CONTENTS

FOREWORD

My mother, Fannie Chamblis Bullock, is my greatest inspiration and role model! She is and will always be. My mother was a teenage mother with twin daughters at the age of 16. Then, she had me at the age of 18. Yes, she had three daughters by 18; yet, she refused to be a statistic. My mother defied the odds, graduated from high school and then college. With the help of my grandparents, she earned her Bachelors' degree and later went on to obtain her Master's degree. My mother made it clear to me and my sisters that education was important and that college was not optional. She made sacrifices and modeled what she expected of us. Because of her determination, my sisters and I all have Bachelor and Master Degrees.

At an early age, I developed a passion for learning and a thirst for knowledge. When I was five, I remember standing at the edge of the driveway waiting eagerly for the yellow school bus to pick me up for my first day of preschool. I wore a circular name tag, made of construction paper that hung from a string made of yarn. I still remember the excitement and anticipation I experienced each morning I went to school. Since that time, I still can't remember a time when I wasn't excited about learning.

In 1993, I was a high school senior at Indian River High School in Chesapeake, Virginia. I began thinking more and more about college. I had a solid academic background. I had a 3.6 grade point average (GPA). I participated in numerous school activities including band, student government, class council, drama club, forensics, literary magazine, and more. In addition, I loved math and science, so I took extra classes including Trigonometry, Pre-Calculus, and Physics. I knew I wanted to become an Engineer. I was book smart but I was not very good at taking standardized aptitude tests, but I knew they were necessary to get accepted into college.

My senior year, I toured several colleges. However, I fell in love with one college in particular: "Hampton University." I distinctly remember visiting Hampton University on High School Day with others from my high school. As our bus approached the campus, I looked out at the beautiful campus and the students walking across campus and thinking that I was at home. The students had an air of distinction about them that I immediately identified with. After the college visit and learning more about Hampton's academic programs, I quickly realized that Hampton University was the college for Me! It was love at first visit. I had just one problem; I could not afford to go to Hampton. It was a private college and the tuition was higher than in-state colleges. The tuition was more than what my parents could afford to pay. After visiting Hampton University, I told my parents Hampton University was my college of choice and that I wanted to major in Electrical Engineering. My mother shared that Hampton University was not affordable and that I should consider going to an in-state college.

I was disappointed but persistent. My mother and I had a long conversation about affordable colleges and Hampton University was not affordable. I was insistent on going to Hampton, but my mother stressed that I would need to find money to attend Hampton or choose a different school…and that was final. In that moment, my life changed because I had no clue about finding college money but I knew that I was going to Hampton University. I was willing to do whatever it took to get accepted and change my financial reality. I had unprecedented determination.

I'll admit, I knew very little about the college admission process or applying for scholarships. I observed my mother as she helped my sisters apply to college but there many things I still did not know. I didn't even know where to start. What I did know is that I needed to get organized and I needed to develop a system to help me stay ahead of deadlines and requirements. I realized I would need to take timely actions to get admitted into Hampton and to find funding. I was not your typical high school scholar. I grew reluctant to rely on my parents to facilitate my college admissions process. It was important for me to take initiative and to lead this effort. Once I knew that I wanted to attend Hampton University, I focused on understanding the college admissions process, obtaining letters of recommendation, writing essays, and finding funding.

During the early 1990s, I did not have access to the Internet. My research efforts took time and useful information required searching. I visited libraries frequently and read books to understand the basics of what I needed to do. Therefore, I knew I needed to develop a systematic approach. I kept piles of documents that I could pull from to simply the college application process. I requested letters of recommendations, wrote essays, and filled out applications ahead of time. I reused essays and application information so that I would not have to reinvent the wheel as I applied for many scholarships. I found numerous scholarships and mailed completed applications off. I tracked which scholarships I applied for. Also, I documented scholarship decisions as I received them. At times, I grew discouraged when I received rejection letters, but I persevered because I knew all I needed was the "right" opportunity or just one "yes."

One key thing I realized was how critical it was to have a good relationship with my high school guidance counselor. I will never forget her. I spent a quite a bit of time in her office sharing my college interests, requesting transcripts, and asking questions about scholarships, financial aid, and other related college admissions aspects. I remember sharing with my guidance counselor that I wanted to major in Electrical Engineering at Hampton University. What I didn't know at the time was how sharing that information with her would change my life.

During a school assembly in the auditorium one day, she pulled me out of the assembly early. We went back to her office and she shared that she ran across a scholarship she thought I would be perfect for. The only challenge was that the deadline to apply for it was in two days. The scholarship was for a student planning to major an engineering at either Hampton University or Virginia Tech. The scholarship recipient(s) would receive a full-tuition scholarship for four years, paid summer internships every summer while attending college, and a full-time engineering job after college graduation.

I wanted that scholarship! There was only one problem with the scholarship, the application had to be postmarked in two days. She asked if I could pull together all the application documentation by the deadline. I told her I would make it happen and I did. I went home, read the application, pulled from the piles of pre-staged documents I accumulated. I revised previous essays and typed up my application (I had a typewriter back then; not a computer). My application was mailed and post marked before the deadline!

Weeks later, I received a letter stating that I was pre-selected as a scholarship finalist to interview for the scholarship. I was excited! Then, I realized that I had never interviewed for anything this important before. I went to the library and checked out a few books on how to interview. I borrowed a black business suit, black dress shoes, and pearl earrings. I practiced interview questions and responses, and came up with several good interview questions to ask. Fortunately, my first interview went so well, I the company invited me to back for a second interview with a panel. After the second interview, I was told the decision would be made in several weeks. However, that same day, I walked in the house after the second interview to the house phone ringing. I nervously answered the phone and received the call from the company that they selected me for the scholarship! I thanked them for the opportunity, hung up, thanked God, and then cried. At that moment, I knew prayer and hard work paid off!

My senior year, I also received several other scholarships. My father served in the U.S. Navy and I received a U.S. Navy/Marine Relief Scholarship. I also received a scholarship from the Gamma Delta Omega Chapter of Alpha Kappa Alpha Sorority, Incorporated. To this day, I am thankful and grateful for the financial assistance! I later became a member of the Gamma Theta Chapter of Alpha Kappa Alpha Sorority, Incorporated in 1998.

I followed my dreams. I attended and graduated from Hampton University with a Bachelor's of Science degree in Electrical Engineering with honors. I later went on to earn two Master's degrees (Computer Information Systems from the University of Phoenix and Business Administration from Strayer University), and a Doctorate in Business Administration from the University of Phoenix.

Fast forward years later, I found myself helping my sons, nieces, nephews, and other children in my community with their college planning efforts. One day I realized that helping other scholars was my passion because I believe in education and continuous learning. Also, I am grateful for those who took the time to help me and that made all the difference in my life. I decided to write this book because someone helped me get to college and I want to help other scholars achieve their college dreams and find money to cover the expenses.

ACKNOWLEDGEMENTS

To my mother, Fannie Chamblis Bullock, my role model, thank you for setting the best example of how I could defy the odds and reach my potential. I appreciate your help editing my book. To my oldest son, Kendall Devon Lewis, thank you for helping me pick this topic. To my youngest son, Kameron Tyrese Lewis, for exceeding my expectations daily and for inspiring me to write about my college planning experiences to assist others. Thank you to my niece Alanna Porter for the opportunity to help with er college planning endeavors that started this all. To my sister Casandra Chamblis and niece Jada Simone Holloway, thank you both for cheerleading me on and for helping with my college planning seminars.

To Felix A. Poteate II, thank you for your continued support. You are the wind beneath my wings. Thank you from the bottom of my heart for being the best friend a woman could ever ask for. I appreciate your support and for believing in me when I didn't know how to believe in myself.

To Hampton University, thank you for providing me with a world-class "Education for Life" and instilling in me an unprecedented "Standard of Excellence." To my executive coaches, Glenn Brome and Dr. Cheryl Jordan (also my sorority sister) thank you for listening to me share my professional aspirations and desire to write my first book. A special thanks to the anonymous individual who gifted me with the book, "*Is there a book inside you? Writing Alone or with a Collaborator,*" by Dan Poynter & Mindy Bingham. This book changed my life and propelled me to action to write my first book. It was easy to read and contained numerous great resources. I highly recommend it to others who have a book inside them, eager to get out.

Finally, to God be the glory. I cannot say thank you enough to God for blessing me in so many ways and for planting seeds of purpose inside me. I thank God for revealing to me how to release my talents and to bury my fears. I also thank God for providing me with such great family, friends, and colleagues. I am certainly grateful for the ability to serve and help others and strength to persevere through the toughest times.

INTRODUCTION

"Education is not the learning of facts, but the training of the mind to think."
Albert Einstein

Deciding to attend and apply to college is a major step in your educational pursuit. Each year, parents and students apply to college and look for funding. Preparing to transition to college can be exciting and be challenging at the same time. While there is an abundance of information available on the Internet, many parents and students find it difficult to navigate the college planning process. This book will assist middle and high school students and parents with this process.

From here on out, this students in this book will be referred to as "**scholars.**" A scholar is defined as a student who seeks to achieve academic excellence through the pursuit of knowledge and understanding. This book is for scholars who have a thirst for knowledge and a desire to attend college to pursue excellence.

Homeschooling

Not all scholars attend a traditional or private high school. According to the National Home Education Research Institute, homeschooling is a parent-led home-based education program. As of 2016, there were over 2.3 million

1

homeschooled students in the U.S. Homeschooling is the fasted growing educational approach in the U.S. and the homeschool population continues to grow, especially with minorities. In most states, homeschooled scholars must register in the state he or she resides.

Parents of homeschooled high school scholars may have the right to decide the courses a child takes to graduate. However, if the parent wishes for the child to attend college, remember that homeschool scholars must meet college entrance requirements as well. Some homeschooled scholars are part of an active home-school community where parents pool their resources together. Each college may have different requirements and documentation for the homeschooled. College admission departments can be very helpful, and some schools have specific information and web pages set up to assist homeschoolers. As you read, this book may offer insights to homeschoolers.

Navigating the College Planning Process

Surprisingly, not all parents and scholars understand the basic steps it takes to get through the college planning process successfully. Some parents and scholars navigate the college planning process easily because they have access to information and resources. These scholars may have access to great support systems or financial resources to assist them. However, do not assume that scholars with strong academic records have it all figured out. I have crossed paths with high school scholars with exceptional academic performance or high aptitude test scores who struggle with the college admissions process and finding college funding. It is unfortunate when high school graduates with a 3.0 grade point average (GPA) or higher failed to attend college because they did not have adequate funding to cover college expenses. Moreover, these examples highlight why parents and scholars could benefit from some practical college planning assistance. In these instances, some scholars struggle to understand how to (1) select a major or career of interest, (2) narrow down college selections, and/or (3) find adequate funding.

There is no secret to college planning. There are plenty of resources, books, videos, and articles on college planning and admissions available on the Internet and in libraries. Yet, numerous scholars and parents still struggle to understand how to apply and find funding for college. Either there is too much college planning information or it is not easy to find the right information in a timely manner. It can be easy to become overwhelmed or frustrated with the process and want to give up. But don't give up!

College Planning Strategies

The intent of this book is to streamline your college planning efforts by: (1) offering useful and practical strategies to apply for and get accepted into colleges, (2) providing key information and resources needed, and (3) taking the mystery and hardship out of the college admissions and planning process. This book will also offer useful templates as resources to maximize your time and effort with college planning so you can focus on the most critical aspects of this process. This book will demystify the secrets of college planning by providing you with college planning strategies to help parents and scholars successfully navigate college admissions processes and find funding:

College Planning Strategies

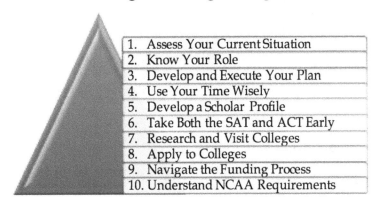

1.	Assess Your Current Situation
2.	Know Your Role
3.	Develop and Execute Your Plan
4.	Use Your Time Wisely
5.	Develop a Scholar Profile
6.	Take Both the SAT and ACT Early
7.	Research and Visit Colleges
8.	Apply to Colleges
9.	Navigate the Funding Process
10.	Understand NCAA Requirements

Templates

This book contains samples and templates, designated by a Template number. Scholars can customize these templates to assist with their college planning efforts. You will not have to develop these from scratch. These templates are available for download online at: https://www.investnothers.com/college-planning.

- Template 1. Where Are You Now Assessment
- Template 2. College Admissions Plan
- Template 3. Scholar Profile
- Template 4. College Selection Factors Level of Importance Spreadsheet
- Template 5. College Requirements Spreadsheet
- Template 6. Scholarship Tracking Spreadsheet
- Template 7. Scholar-Athlete Profile

Whether you are starting as early as middle school, as a freshman in high school, or as a high school senior, the information in this book will prove to be valuable in your college planning endeavors. The content of this book is comprehensive enough to reduce the amount of time spent researching basic information. The purpose of this book is to highlight information from various sources in one place to streamline the time it takes you to find the information you need.

Since you are reading this book, you have an interest in planning for college or helping someone plan for college and/or find money to pay for college. You do not have much time to waste, and you probably want to cut to the chase and get down to business. If so, then this book is for you. The practical strategies, templates, and resources contained in this book will offer you a roadmap to navigate the college application process. If you like to plan ahead and prepare for college, this book will provide you the best college preparation and funding advice.

STRATEGY 1: ASSESS YOUR CURRENT SITUATION

"...it's important to do an honest and accurate self-assessment of your abilities." Travis Bradberry

As you begin this college planning journey, it is necessary that you honestly assess the scholar's current situation. It is imperative to get a sense of the scholar's current academic situation and a sense of his or her future college aspirations. Understanding where you are currently can help accelerate the scholar's college planning progress. This may sound like a strange strategy; however, just go with it.

College planning is similar to taking a trip by car across the country. Map out your journey by determining where you want to go, estimating how long the trip will take, and identifying the best route, and understanding whether or not you will need money for tolls. You must know your starting point to reach your desired destination.

Applying this strategy will help you to establish a baseline or a reference point for where you are now in the college planning process and what actions you still need to take to achieve your college admission goals. Establishing a baseline is assessing the scholar's current academic performance, course workload, knowledge of available resources, and initial college aspirations.

Where Are You Now Assessment

To start, I recommend that you take five minutes and complete the *Where Are You Now Assessment* (**Template 1**) without looking for information, asking others, or putting a lot of thought into it. Think of this assessment as a pop-quiz or pre-test. It will provide useful insight into your college planning process in ways you might not have considered.

If you are a parent or guardian, complete the *Where Are You Now Assessment* based on your knowledge of the scholar you are helping. Write down what you understand about your child or scholar. If you are a middle or high school scholar, complete the assessment based on your current academic situation. Answer all the questions you can honestly and skip over those you are unable to answer. If you do not know the answer off the top of your head, simply leave it blank. I would caution you not to get discouraged. This assessment is merely to help you identify gaps and opportunities to improve your college planning outlook. So, start by asking yourself these questions:

Where Are You Now Assessment

1. What is your (child/scholar's) cumulative GPA? _____

2. True or False. Only scholars with a high GPA get scholarships? _____

3. What is your Guidance Counselor's name?

   _____

4. What is the process for obtaining your transcripts at your high school?

   _____

5. True or False. You should apply for college in the Spring of your senior year.

   _____

6. What are your top *three* college/university choices?

   _____

   _____

7. What are the top *three* college majors you are considering?

   _____

   _____

8. True or False. Most colleges prefer SAT scores over ACT scores. _____

9. True or False. Average grades in hard courses are better than A's in easy courses.

   _____

10. True or False. Your social media activity will not influence your college admission selection. _____

Where Are You Now Assessment Responses

After you complete the assessment, take a few minutes to review the responses for each question. If your responses to the *Where Are You Now Assessment* questions seemed painful, then this book is undoubtedly for you. Here are some considerations for each question:

1. What is your (child/scholar's) current cumulative GPA?

If you did not know the scholar's current GPA, you may limit your ability to improve the scholar's academic record before applying to colleges or applying for merit-based scholarships.

2. True or False. Only scholars with high GPAs get scholarships.

False. This is a myth. Not all scholarships are merit-based or geared toward scholars with high GPAs or athletes. With a bit of effort and diligence, scholars can minimize the cost of paying for school. There are numerous scholarship resources available online (i.e., www.scholly.com) and other sources that advertise scholarship merit-based, program areas, community-based religions, organization affiliations, and more. I have assisted numerous scholars whose GPAs were 2.5 and above receive full tuition scholarships. Sometimes, these individuals have multiple scholarship offers to help with room and board, books, and more. The key is to continuously look for opportunities through your local churches, businesses, corporations, universities, and social/civic organizations.

3. What is your Guidance Counselor's name?

Guidance Counselors can offer great support and can provide you with a wealth of information and resources as you plan. Not to mention, guidance counselors will likely be your best resource to understand specific high school processes and systems you will probably need access to request transcripts and letters of recommendations.

4. What is the process for obtaining your transcripts at your high school?

Each school's transcript request process may be different. Take time to learn what that process is for your school before you need to request transcripts. Some schools require permissions, waivers, and other forms to be complete. In some cases, it may take time to get these documents processed, so it will be crucial to know what this process is before you have short-term deadlines to request and submit transcripts.

5.   True or False. The best time to apply for college is in the Spring of your senior year.

False. You should apply in the Summer after your junior year or Fall of your senior year. If you are starting to apply for college in the Spring of your senior year, you are behind in the admission process and potentially losing out on scholarships and financial aid funding opportunities.

6.   What are your top <u>three</u> college/university choices?

Narrowing down your top three college/university choices may require you conducting some research and college visits. If you are not already thinking about it, you should begin thinking about potential majors and programs of interest to ensure that your top colleges have the programs you are interested in.   Other factors might include location, tuition costs, and quality of academic programs.

7.   What are your top <u>three</u> college majors for consideration?

Selecting college majors and areas of study will require you to explore your interests, fields of study, and possible career choices. You may also want to research colleges/universities to see if they offer the programs of interest as you narrow down your search.

8. True or False. Most colleges and universities prefer SAT scores over ACT scores.

False. Not necessarily. Some colleges accept both test scores, while others might prefer SAT or ACT scores. At the same time, some colleges require no SAT or ACT scores unless the scholar is interested in applying for university scholarships.

9. True or False. Average grades in hard classes are better than A's in easy ones. True. It is better to take more challenging courses and get a B, than it is to take an easier course. Colleges like to see scholars challenge themselves and take more difficult courses. If you are not a senior, consider scheduling your course load by taking more difficult courses that will prepare you for college and help you to differentiate yourself from other scholars seeking college admissions.

10. True or False. Your social media activity will not influence your college admission selection.

False. When I attended college in the late 90s, the Internet and social media was not a factor. However, social media is prevalent and how you "show up" online or on social media sites…it all matters. College admissions representatives, recruiters, coaches, and other affiliates may conduct searches to get a better idea of how a prospective scholar conducts themselves on social media and factor that into their admission decision.

To navigate the college planning journey successfully, it is imperative that you assess your current academic situation and understand where you are to maximize how you spend your time. By completing the *Where Are You Now Assessment,* you should have a better understanding of your current academic performance gaps you need to close, and opportunities to improve your college admission chances. If you were unable to answer any questions, explore your shortcomings and work to address them. As you continue to read this book, you will gain strategies and techniques to help you strengthen your academic performance and address identified gaps.

The goal of this assessment is for you to start thinking about what you need to do to prepare for college and getting admitted. You should spend time understanding your academic performance, high school transcript processes, college application requirements and processes, and etc. For example, in 2014, I assisted my niece in applying to college. She needed her high school transcript to submit with several college applications. She quickly learned that because she did not know her high school's transcript request process in advance, it took longer for her high school to send her transcripts to colleges. It is very essential not to allow others (including your school, guidance counselor, or teacher) to become your critical path or hold up to getting your college and scholarship applications submitted ahead of deadlines. You need to stay two steps ahead by fully understanding the process so that your applications thorough, complete, and timely.

Knowing your GPA matters. Don't wait until your senior year to find out your GPA, because you will be unlikely to make significant improvements to your GPA (if needed) to improve your odds of getting accepted into the schools you want or qualifying for specific funding or scholarships. Athletes who want to play collegiate sports should know their GPA and academic standing throughout high school so that they do not jeopardize their collegiate athletic eligibility status.

STRATEGY 2: KNOW YOUR ROLE

"If everyone is moving forward together, then success takes care of itself." Henry Ford

As you consider how to navigate the college planning process strategically, make sure you know your role as a parent/guardian and as a scholar. By consciously focusing on your role, you will make significant progress in achieving your college admission outcomes. To effectively achieve college plans, it will be essential for parents and scholars to identify and agree on roles and responsibilities clearly.

Parent and Guardian Roles and Responsibilities

There are specific things that parents can do to impact their scholar's success and increase their odds of getting accepted into college and finding financial resources. Consider the following parent/guardian college planning roles:

Parent/Guardian Roles and Responsibilities

- Take an Active Role
- Keep an Open Mind
- Do Your Own Research
- Develop a Relationship with School Officials
- Know What's Going On Academically
- Take Your Child to Visit Colleges
- Budget for College Expenses
- Encourage Your Child to Stay On Track

Take an Active Role

Take an active role in helping to navigate college planning endeavors. Your active participation in the college planning process will be critical. Please do not solely rely on teachers, guidance counselors, and/or coaches for assistance. They are likely assisting numerous students at a time. You are best positioned to provide dedicated support to your child/scholar. A scholar's high school years are critical and these years will go by fast. Invest in your child/scholar, from grades K through 12, and follow them through the process until they get accepted in the college of their choice and have adequate funding.

Offer support to child throughout the process and remain diligent. The junior or senior year of high school is not the time when parents should leave such a critical college

17

planning process up to high school scholars. For example, I met a couple with children in high school. I asked how their high school children were doing with college preparation. The parents were frustrated because their son applied to college and struggled to find financial aid other than student loans. When I asked what actions were they taking to support their son find more funding, the father shrugged his shoulders and said, "I don't know... it's up to him at this point. He is at a point where he needs to figure it out for himself."

Initially, the father's response surprised me. But, I had heard similar sentiments from other parents who believed it was their child's responsibility to drive this process if they wanted to attend college. The problem with this philosophy is that the child may not know what they do not know. Whether the parent admits it or not, your child will still need help and support. Remain involved and support your child or scholar from beginning to end.

Keep an Open Mind

Keep an open mind about your child's college aspirations. Your child will likely need encouragement and guidance to understand and research college requirements, potential areas of study, careers, financial aid options, and more. Keep an open mind and allow your child to explore his or her aspirations and interests with an open mind. You may not agree with your child's intended areas of study, college choice, the location from home, the high cost of tuition, and other factors. However, prematurely exerting strong opinions, limitations, or directives might damper your child's interest in college altogether.

Do Your Own Research

Preparing for college will require you to find out as much information as possible to support your child effectively. While the Internet contains a wealth of college planning information, the information is not streamlined or synthesized in a manner that allows you to get your hands on what you need to know quickly. Conducting research and finding out necessary information will allow you to better support your child through the process. When you find useful information, keep a file or repository of website links and other documents so you can reference them in the future easily. Table A contains examples of topics to research and learn more.

Table A: College Planning Research Topics

Admission Requirements	College Testing Types	Funding Sources
Application Processes	SAT vs ACT	Financial Aid Processes
College Visits and Tours	SAT (Dates, Fees, Register)	Scholarships
Majors and Programs	Prep Courses	Grants
Tuition and Fees	NCAA Eligibility Requirements	Student Loans

As you research these college planning topics, you may find other areas of interest that you will want to research. Explore the new topics also. Take notes on relevant information and facts that you may not have previously been exposed to or information that you do not want to forget.

Develop a Relationship with School Counselors

Develop a solid relationship with high school officials, especially your child's guidance counselor. Depending on your high school's organizational structure, your child's guidance counselor may be assigned by your child's grade level or by your child's last name. Some high schools assign a guidance counselor to your child from grades 9 through 12. If you have not already done so, arrange a time to visit your child's high school to meet key school officials.

These relationships will be extremely important. Know

key officials by name, get their contact information, and visit with them periodically to discuss your child's courses, academic performance, future course schedule, diploma requirements, college aspirations, local high school/college joint programs, and transcript request processes. Guidance counselors and other high school officials provide valuable resources and services to scholars and parents on diploma requirements, graduation activities, upcoming events and workshops, and other informational opportunities.

Know What's Going on Academically

Know what's going on academically with grades, GPA, test scores, activities, and timelines. As you meet with relevant school officials, such as your child's guidance counselor, make sure you find out how to access your child's (1) grade point average, (2) test scores, (3) grades, and (4) school assignments. Many schools use online portals that allow parents to log in with a username and password to access this information. Check your child's GPA after each semester.

The goal is to stay on top of this information so that you do not get to your child's junior or senior year and find out your child's academic performance is not where you thought it would be. Verifying academic progress, early and often, gives you and your child an opportunity to change courses and influence your outcomes when needed. Also, if your child desires to attend a particular college, it would be helpful to know how well your child will meet that college's admissions requirements.

Take Your Child to Visit Colleges

Before your child selects or narrows down colleges to attend, it is imperative to visit different colleges before making a decision. There are different types of college tours you could take: open houses, self-guided tours, walking tours, virtual tours, and overnight visits. When my sons were younger, we would visit colleges whenever we traveled. We took self-guided tours to expose them to colleges. We enjoyed exploring campuses at our own pace. At times, we would visit colleges while school was in session and the boys were able to talk to scholars and to get a feel for what it was like to attend that school.

Budget for College Expenses

Budget for college planning expenses. Examples of expenses to consider include: college application fees, travel costs for college visits, SAT/ACT registration fees, and SAT/ACT prep courses. Planning for college admissions means there are fees, costs, and expenses that you should be aware of. You should anticipate what your expenses might be each year and budget for them based on your college planning strategies. Each year, identify college planning actions you and your child will execute and determine how much each activity may cost.

Encourage Your Child

Since the entire college planning process can be overwhelming, some youth may need more encouragement than others. Whether you attended college or not, be positive and encouraging. Education is a gateway to more opportunity; therefore, anything you can do and say to encourage your child will be fruitful. Encourage your child to stay on track and monitor progress. One of the most important things you can do to support your child is to encourage him or her to stay focused and follow through. There will be competing demands for time and if not careful, months and years can go by, and your child might miss important deadlines and timeframes that might help position them well. Once you and your child identify college planning action, review your progress monthly and adjust your plans based on your reality.

Scholar Roles and Responsibilities

No one is more important in this process than the scholars. In fact, scholars are ultimately responsible and accountable for the success and outcomes of their college planning efforts. If the scholar commits to putting forth an effort and taking the lead in this process, he or she will be extremely pleased with the results. The entire college planning process will provide an opportunity for scholars to demonstrate that they are willing to do what it takes to secure their future and that they are serious about attending college. The college planning process presents a natural opportunity for scholars to learn more about courses, requirements, colleges, expenses, and handling business. Consider the following scholar roles and responsibilities:

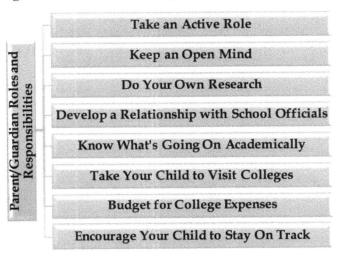

Own the Process and Work Hard

Own the college planning process and prepare to work hard. Scholars will need to multi-task. College planning activities and actions will likely take place while scholars are attending high school, playing sports, working part-time, and participating in other activities. Scholars should understand that they will work hard, sacrifice their time, and take necessary actions at critical times to best position themselves. No one will have more at stake than the scholar does; therefore, the scholar should get in the driver's seat, buckle up, and prepare for the journey!

Keep Your Grades Up

Take your academic achievement serious and strive to achieve the best possible grade you can in every class or course. Scholars are taking high school courses as early as middle school, and it matters how well you perform in all high school courses because they will affect your high school GPA. Academic performance is the key to unlocking endless opportunities!

I spoke with a 6th-grade middle school scholar. She expressed to me that she loved Math but hated Science. I shared with her that just because you hate Science, it does not mean you cannot be good at it and excel. After her first semester in 6th grade, she shared her report card with me, and sure enough, she achieved an A in both Math and Science. In fact, she had mostly A's on that report card with only a couple B's. The point is, there will always be courses and subjects that you will find more exciting and interesting than others; but, it does not mean that the other courses do not deserve equal attention or that that you cannot excel in less interesting courses.

Similarly, college admission professionals also like to see scholars challenge themselves by taking Advance Placement (AP) courses. Scholars should consider the AP courses but not at the expense of struggling academically and risking a low GPA. Talk with your parents and guidance counselor to determine the best academic courses for you. Every scholar may be different so do not be afraid to make adjustments based on your needs and performance.

At the same time, as you work to achieve the best academic performance you can, plan to verify and record your GPA after every semester. Why might this be important? It is important because as a scholar, you cannot improve or make changes when you do not know what your current academic situation is. You may need time to pull up that grade before receiving your final report card. You may decide you need extra help, to seek out a tutor, turn in extra work for extra credit, or identify other improvement options.

<u>Get Involved in School/Community Activities</u>

Scholars must be able to balance academics and participation in other activities. Get involved in school and community activities during middle school and high school. Many college admission professions want to admit scholars who are well-rounded and balanced in classroom and in the community. There are numerous ways to get involved in other activities.

Whether you play sports, sing, perform liberal arts, volunteer in the community, or other activities, the goal is to get involved and show diversity. Additionally, take advantage of opportunities to step up and take on a leadership role in some activities. College admissions professionals make admission determinations based on scholars who show that they have leadership capabilities. As you participate in activities, scholars should track the dates they participated, and the membership/positions held so that they can easily refer back to these experiences when needed. Also, as you participate, identify adults who may be able to write you a future letter of recommendation. Get their contact information (organization name, title, phone number, and email address) early on so that you can revisit with them later.

Spend Time on College Aspirations

Spend time considering your future college aspirations as early as middle school. Depending on what grade you are in as a scholar, you might have more time or less time to consider your options. The early you start thinking about these things, the better research you can do and the more satisfied you will be final selections and college choices. Scholars should spend time thinking about important decisions such as your:

- Career, college major, or areas of study interests?
- Top 5-6 colleges/universities?
- College admission requirements and eligibility of your top schools?
- Areas or states would you prefer?
- College expenses and fees required?

When scholars consider these questions, and begin to shape what their preferences and desires are, the easier it will be for others to assist them in the college planning process. These considerations will lead to more focused and targeted research to find colleges/universities, majors and programs of interest, and a variety of funding resources that might be good fits for the scholar.

Use the Internet for Research

Use the Internet for more than social media. Do some research! Take advantage of the Internet and the easy access to information to help with your college planning pursuits. I went through the college planning process back in the 1990s, and unfortunately, I did not have the benefit of the Internet to assist me. Therefore, my research process took more time, and it was a bit more difficult finding information. Fortunately, technology advancements have made it easier to access the information you need, relatively fast. Make the most of having information at your fingertips and do some research yourself. Throughout this book, references to the Internet and online sources will be provided.

Ask for Help

Don't' be afraid to ask for help. Scholars might become overwhelmed with the entire college planning endeavor. There are numerous steps to take and a lot of information to understand. It will be important for scholars not to get discouraged or spin their wheels at critical points without making progress. Information and resources are available to assist scholars, but it will up to the scholar to ask for timely assistance. Also, scholars should be proactive and ask questions to ensure they have a good understanding of what processes and steps they may need to take.

Don't Waste People's Time

Time is a valuable commodity. It should not be wasted. Wasting other people's time is one of my pet peeves. Throughout the college planning process, a scholar may receive support from others such as parents, relatives, teachers, other school officials, coaches, friends, community organizers, and many others. As scholars seek assistance with college applications, essay reviews, letters of recommendations and more, remember that these individuals are doing you a favor; not the other way around. Be responsive and diligent when requesting assistance and follow-up promptly.

For example, a high school senior asked me to write a letter of recommendation for her college application package. I agreed to write a letter for her, and I asked her to provide me information on her background, courses she took, extracurricular activities, college aspirations and more. I asked her to provide this information within a week. I waited a week and never received the requested information. I emailed her to find out the status. She responded two days later. When others are helping, realize that they are not on your timeline…you are on theirs. Respect people's time.

STRATEGY 3: DEVELOP AND EXECUTE YOUR PLAN

"Education is the passport to the future, for tomorrow belongs to those who prepare for it today." Malcolm X

Developing an effective college plan can accelerate your progress and increase your chances of getting admitted into the colleges of your choice and finding funding to cover tuition and expenses. A plan will serve as the roadmap to guide you through the college planning process. Once you have established a plan, you can set goals, estimate costs, and create a realistic schedule.

College Admissions Plan

Your *College Admissions Plan* (**Template 2**) should be customized to fit your specific situation. At a minimum, your plan should include the necessary information such as a list of actions to take, cost/expenses, the time frame to complete the actions, and a status update. In fact, your college admissions plan should be grade level specific. Tailor the college admissions plan for middle school and high school scholars. Table B depicts a sample college admissions plan to help you begin. A full college admissions plan can be downloaded online.

Table B: Sample College Admissions Plan

	College Admissions Plan (Year = Rising 10TH Grade)						
	My Goals	**Type**	**Cost**	**Start Date**	**Due Date**	**% Complete**	**Notes**
1	Develop a *Scholar Profile*	Profile	N/A	Summer before 10th grade	Summer before 10th grade	75%	Use the *Scholar Profile*
2	Research colleges and requirements	College	N/A	Summer before 10th grade	Summer before 10th grade	25%	Use the *College Requirement Spreadsheet*
3	Meet Guidance Counselor	High School	N/A	9/15/XX	9/30/XX	25%	Scheduled for 9/20/XX
4	Find out your current GPA and get a copy of your transcript	High School	N/A	9/20/XX	10/1/XX	0%	
5	Schedule to take the SAT and ACT	Test	$65.00	2/01/XX	4/01/XX	0%	

- Schedule a meeting with your school Guidance Counselor:

  o Understand the high school graduation requirements for each diploma program early. A meeting will help scholars determine which diploma program they might be interested in pursuing.

o   Discuss your high school course requirements and college interests. Review the course schedule for middle school and high school. Determine what courses your scholar will take each year. In fact, some scholars begin taking high school courses as early as middle school. Adjust the courses after each school year. Encourage your scholar to consider taking challenging courses to test his or her capabilities and to boost their confidence.

o   Obtain a copy of your high school transcript and know your GPA. Plan on getting an updated transcript after each semester to track your academic progress. Review your transcript for errors and opportunities. Periodic reviews will allow you time to correct mistakes and strategically plan your future course load to help you meet high school graduation and college admission requirements. Also, find out the official process for obtaining letters of recommendation ahead of time. When you begin applying for colleges and scholarships you want to make sure requesting transcripts will not delay your application timing.

- Establish and maintain sound study habits will be helpful skills to develop early. These skills will benefit scholars through high school and college. It is a critical period because scholars will be establishing sound study habits and identifying high school courses they seek to take. If your scholar struggles with homework and study habits, consider getting him or her some help.

- Get involved in extracurricular and community activities. Scholars might enjoy engaging with others and identifying new interests they may have. Many college and university admission administrators like to see well-rounded scholars apply to college. Scholars can have high grades, but colleges want to know that they were involved in other activities, lead organizations, and volunteered in their communities.

- Track school work and academic progress and performance regularly. Keep up with your scholar's homework, test, and project assignments. Encourage your child to complete extra credit assignments also. Monitoring progress allows you and the scholar time to make the necessary adjustments and corrections before the grading period ends. Also, celebrate incremental successes along the way to keep your scholar motivated and encouraged.

- Research college and university requirements.
    - Make a list of college requirements, career interests, programs offered, and possible college majors.
    - Identify colleges of interest and begin visiting colleges and universities in your community and when you plan vacations and trips to other places. Visit colleges you think your scholars may be interested in and those they may not be interested in. The goal is to expose them to a broad array of college and university campuses and programs.
- Schedule and register to take the SAT **and** ACT.
- Get facts about current tuition cost and expenses and begin establishing a plan to pay for college. Start thinking about financial aid and scholarships. College can be affordable but it will require doing some research to understand high education costs.

Getting Organized

Get organized. At the same time, getting organized will be important throughout this college planning process. Organization is an important skill to have for college. Scholars should develop a system to organize (1) electronic files, (2) hard copy paperwork, and (3) login usernames and passwords and more.

The best way to do this is to spend a few minutes developing a system or approach that works best for the scholar. Here are some examples for your consideration:

Electronic or Paper Copy Filing System:

Another aspect of planning is getting organized on your computer. Establish an electronic folder system for current and future materials with a naming convention (with the date you stored them) to help you intuitively find documents information easily. Store and save documents in the same places consistently. Consider the example naming and organizational computer files convention in Table C:

Table C: Computer Folder Structure

Folder Name	Subfolders' Names
High School	<ul><li>Transcripts</li><li>Report Cards</li><li>School Schedules</li><li>School Official Contact Information</li><li>Guidance Counselor Contact Information</li><li>Graduation Requirements</li><li>Photos (for applications and test registrations)</li><li>Login for school accounts</li></ul>
Scholar Profile	<ul><li>***Scholar Profile***</li><li>Extracurricular activities</li><li>Awards and Honors (certificates)</li><li>Job Employment Experiences</li><li>References</li></ul>
SAT/ACT Tests	<ul><li>SAT<ul><li>Registration, Dates, and Fees</li><li>School Codes</li><li>Score Results</li><li>Prep Courses</li></ul></li><li>ACT<ul><li>Registration, Dates, and Fees</li><li>School Codes</li><li>Score Results</li><li>Prep Courses</li></ul></li></ul>
Letters of Recommendations	<ul><li>Sample Letters of Recommendation</li><li>Points of Contact</li><li>Completed Letters of Recommendations<ul><li>College Applications</li><li>Scholarship Applications</li></ul></li></ul>
Essays	<ul><li>College Applications</li><li>Scholarship Applications</li></ul>
Colleges	<ul><li>College Research<ul><li>Requirements and Eligibility</li><li>Tuition and Fees</li><li>Tracking Sheet</li></ul></li><li>College Visits/Tours</li><li>Applications<ul><li>College X Name<ul><li>Application</li><li>Letters of Recommendations</li><li>Essays</li></ul></li></ul></li></ul>

A solid college admissions plan can and getting organized can make all the difference. By establishing a plan, the process will seem less overwhelming. Additionally, you can manage your time and resources (including money) more effectively and track progress easily. Developing a college admissions plan and a system for your files will position scholars and parents to understand high school challenges and college requirements better early on. Help your scholar set goals and stay focused.

STRATEGY 4: USE YOUR TIME WISELY

"This is the key to time management - to see the value of every moment." Menachem Mendel Schneerson

Timing is everything! Use your time wisely by planning early and executing. It is never too early to begin planning and taking action. From my experiences assisting with college planning, timing is the one factor that impacts college admission success and finding funding. Do not wait until your senior year of high school to begin this process. You may miss out on opportunities to do the following: (1) influence or improve your GPA and grades, (2) improve SAT and/or ACT scores, (3) research college requirements better, (4) draft essays in advance, (5) identify individuals for references, (6) strategically apply for colleges, and (7) maximize funding opportunities.

As early as middle school, take advantage of all the opportunities to plan and execute your goals promptly. There are things you can accomplish to better position yourself each year of middle school and high school for college and beyond. Develop and execute a timeline for each school year and align it with your college admissions plan. Figure X shows the recommended timeline actions to take for each school year.

39

Timeline Checklist (Grades 8 - 9)

- Understand your high school graduation requirements

- Actively manage your course schedule

- Keep grades up (3.0 GPA & above)

- Review your high school transcript

- Get involved in activities (sports, clubs, community)

- Think about college majors or fields of study

- Develop a Scholar profile

- Research colleges (programs, requirements, costs)

- Research types of scholarships

Timeline Checklist (Grade 10)

- Actively manage your course schedule

- Keep grades up (3.0 GPA & above)

- Review your high school transcript

- Stay involved in activities (sports, clubs, community)

- Think about college majors or fields of study

- Research colleges (programs, requirements, costs)

- Visit colleges

- Update your Scholar profile

- Take the PSAT/SAT/ACT

- Research types of scholarships

- Identify who can write letters of recommendations

- Athletes Only
- Develop a Scholar-Athlete Profile
- Develop your NCAA Certification Profile

Timeline Checklist (Grade 11)

- Verify meeting your high school graduation requirements are met
- Actively manage your course schedule
- Keep grades up (3.0 GPA & above)
- Review your high school transcript
- Find out the transcript request process at your school
- Stay involved in activities (sports, clubs, community)
- Narrow down college majors or fields of study
- Research colleges (programs, requirements, costs)
- Visit colleges
- Update your Scholar Profile
- Take the SAT **and** ACT
- Research financial aid and scholarships
- Identify who can write letters of recommendations
- Athletes only
- Develop a Scholar-Athlete Profile
- Update your NCAA Certification Account (Div I/DivII)
- Send high school transcripts to NCAA Eligibility Center

Timeline Checklist (Grade 12)

- Actively manage your course schedule
- Keep grades up (3.0 GPA & above)
- Review your high school transcript
- Find out the transcript request process at your school
- Sign permission forms to obtain your high school transcript sent out
- Stay involved in activities (sports, clubs, community)
- Select a college major or field of study
- Select your top 5 colleges
- Request official transcripts
- Write college essays (if applicable)
- Obtain letters of recommendation
- Apply to colleges and track results
- Update your Scholar Profile
- Take or re-take the SAT **and** ACT (by October)
- Apply for scholarships and track results
- Complete the Free Application for Federal Student Aid (FAFSA) - online (send results to top 3-5 schools)
- Athletes only
- Develop a Scholar-Athlete Profile
- Update your NCAA Certification Account (Div I/DivII)

- Send high school transcripts to NCAA Eligibility Center (September of 12th grade year)
- Send final transcripts to NCAA Eligibility Center (End of 12th grade year)

STRATEGY 5: DEVELOP A SCHOLAR PROFILE

"The only competition worthy of a wise man is with himself."
Washington Allston

Preparing for college presents an opportunity for you to market yourself so that you can differentiate yourself from others. Marketing yourself means highlighting your best qualities and leveraging your strengths. Colleges and universities will receive applications from scholars across the country and around the world. First impressions are lasting impressions. You have a unique opportunity to determine how you want to show up on paper. Develop a *Scholar Profile* to market yourself and to help others learn more about you in a one-page summary. This document is similar to a resume, but it is different. The *Scholar Profile* seeks to tell the high school story of "you" and highlight your talents and abilities. Developing a *Scholar Profile* can help you market yourself in numerous ways:

- College Applications – You can use the Scholar Profile to fill in vital information on a college application. Developing a completed Scholar Profile will make it easier for you to recall relevant details from events that took place over time. At the same time, some college applications may allow you to attach the Scholar Profile to your application. This will help you to stand out from other college applicants.

- Letters of Recommendation – As you request letters of recommendation, you can provide your Scholar Profile to the individual (guidance counselor, teacher, employer, coach, mentor, etc.) writing a letter of recommendation. Whether the person writing the letter of recommendation is familiar with you or not, the Scholar Profile will help them to know you differently, and it will make it easier for them to write a letter of recommendation for you.

- Scholarship Applications – The *Scholar Profile* is also useful to complete scholarship applications. Besides, it can also be attached to scholarship applications to help you stand out from other scholarship applicants.

Depicted in the *Sample Scholar Profile* (**Template 3**) is a simple Microsoft Word document that tells others who you are, what your goals are, and what you have accomplished. Use the *Scholar Profile* template provided online to tailor it to your interests and experiences.

Sample Scholar Profile

SCHOLAR PROFILE

John Doe
12345 College Bound Drive
City, State Zip Code
Home: (123) 456-789; Mobile: (123) 911-4111
Email: john.doe@yahoo.com

Objective: To attend XX university and obtain a degree in XX.

Education: **High School**: XX High School, City, State (Graduation: 06/13/20XX)
Current GPA: 3.6; Rank: 29/283
ACT Scores: Composite: 24; English (24); Math (30); Reading (21); Science (20)
College Plan: Hampton University (Accepted on 1/20/20XX)
Enrollment Date: Fall 2018
Intended Degree/Major: Bachelor of XX in XX

Honors and Awards:
- Honor Roll, (20XX - Present)
- National Honor Society Induction, 20XX
- Top Alternate Current/Direct Current Student, (20XX-20XX)

Employment Experience:
- Cashier, McDonalds, City, VA (20XX-20XX)
- Walmart Cashier, City, VA (20XX)

Student Organizations/Extracurricular Activities:
- Student Government Association Class Representative, (20XX-Present)
- National Honor Society, (20XX-Present)
- Future Business Leaders of America Member, (20XX-20XX)

Community Service Activities:
- Alpha Kappa Alpha Sorority, Incorporated, Adopt a Highway Project, (20XX)
- Volunteered at Galleria Mall on Summer Family Nights, (20XX)
- Volunteered at the XX Community Center, (20XX)

Relevant Courses:
- Algebra II
- Graphics Design I
- Oceanography

Interests/Hobbies:

- Cooking
- Reading

At a minimum, a *Scholar Profile* should include the following:

- A professional photo (optional) – Include a professional photo of yourself. If you do not have a professional photo, take one with a suit on or a simple solid dress or white shirt and tie on. Your photo should help you set a good first impression. Providing a photo is optional. In some cases, photos may be used to discriminate against applicants or candidates. If you have concerns that adding your photo may not be helpful or that it may be used to discriminate against you, do not include one.

- Name, address, email, and phone numbers – Provide your contact information. Use your name and not a nickname. Also, use an appropriate email address that does not distract from your official business purpose (to get into college or get a scholarship).

- Objective (for college) – Provide a concise statement that tells the reader more about your college aspirations. Consider sharing what type of college you are interested in, what program or major you wish to study, and other relevant information.

- Educational history (summary) – Specify the high school you attend, the address, your GPA, and your anticipated graduation date. Also, specify your SAT/ACT results.
- Honors and awards – List your academic, extra-curricular, and athletic honors and awards. Specify the year you received them. List your most current honor/award first and list the remaining honors/awards in descending order, by date.
- Employment history – Specify your job or employment history. College admission professionals like to see if a student is well-rounded and has a work ethic. List your most current job first and list the remaining experiences in descending order, by date.
- Student organizations/extra-curricular activities – List student organizations and other extra-curricular activities you have taken since your freshman year. Specify if you were a member or if you held a leadership role. List your most current activity first and list the remaining activities in descending order, by date.
- Community service activities – Specify any community service or volunteer work you participated in since your freshman year. List your most current activity first and list the remaining activities in descending order, by date.

College admission professionals like to see students serving their communities.

- Relevant coursework – List relevant courses and/or challenging courses you have taken, like AP courses. Specify courses you took that might highlight why you might be a good fit for a particular college program. For example, if you are interested in an engineering program, you might highlight math, science, and technical courses taken. Do not list every course on your high school transcript.

- Interests/hobbies – Include any hobbies or interests you have that might be useful to include.

When you first develop your *Scholar Profile*, you may notice there may be gaps in some areas. The earlier you develop a *Scholar Profile* in high school years, the more time you will have to address any gaps you may have. You will have time to improve your GPA, participate in clubs and activities, take on leadership roles, volunteer in your community, adjust to take more rigorous courses, or retake the SAT or ACT to improve your score. Understand that as you develop a *Scholar Profile*, you will revise it often. Each time you review your *Scholar Profile,* you will find that you need to update information because you will new accomplishments, experiences, courses, and activities to include.

A *Scholar Profile* will help differentiate you from potential competition. It will also help you organize your accomplishments and tell the story of you. When you apply to colleges and for scholarships, the last thing you want is to spend unnecessary time attempting to recall details included on your *Scholar Profile*. Developing and updating your *Scholar Profile* will save you tremendous time and energy.

You can also check with your high school guidance counseling department for similar resources. Some high school officials have seniors complete a Self-Assessment Form that contains some of the same information included on the *Scholar Profile*. You can provide the Self-Assessment Form or *Scholar Profile* to teachers/administrators who may write letters of recommendations for students.

STRATEGY 6: TAKE BOTH TESTS: SAT AND ACT

"Sometimes the hurdles aren't really hurdles at all. They're welcome challenges, tests." Paul Walker

High school scholars should take both the nationally recognized Scholastic Aptitude Test (SAT) and the American College Testing (ACT) test in their junior year or early in their senior year. These tests are part of the freshman entry college admissions and/or merit-based scholarship process. Colleges refer to these tests as college entrance exams that assess high school scholars' readiness for college entry. These tests measure what a scholar learned in high school and to assess a scholar's preparedness for college.

Homeschooled scholars should also plan to take the SAT and/or ACT because college officials will consider these test results when making admissions decisions. In many states, homeschooled scholars are required to take standardized tests. It may be valuable for middle and high school scholars to begin taking content subject tests so that they become familiar with the college experience. Some colleges place greater emphasis on standardized tests for homeschooled applicants than traditional high school applicants.

51

Both the SAT and ACT follow strict guidelines and time frames. The scores from these tests, along with a scholar's high school GPA, class rank, extra-curricular activities, letters of recommendations, and personal essays may be indicators of a scholar's success in college. The higher the scholar scores on the SAT and/or ACT, the more college admission and scholarship options the scholar will have.

As scholars conduct research and learn more about college admission requirements, pay close attention to the school's SAT and ACT score requirements. The SAT is more popular on the East and West coasts, while the ACT more common in Southern, Midwestern, and Rocky Mountain areas of the U.S. Currently, the ACT is growing in popularity on the East Coast.

Most four-year colleges and universities will accept scores from either the SAT or ACT; however, some colleges place a different emphasis on one test or the other. Also, some colleges do not require either one. It is still a good practice to take one or both of these tests because colleges and universities still use the scores to determine merit-based scholarship eligibility. Also, athletes who intend to play National Collegiate Athletic Association (NCAA) sports, will need to take one of these tests to qualify for NCAA eligibility.

SAT

The SAT is created and published by the College Board, a private, non-profit organization in the U.S. Originally, the SAT did not align with high school curricula; however, in 2016, the College Board redesigned the test to closely align with what students actually learn in high school. The SAT measures how well students analyze and problem solve. The SAT score is calculated based on the number of questions answered correctly. There is no penalty for guessing on the SAT. All SAT questions are weighted equally.

Students will receive a separate score on a 200 to 800-point scale for the: (1) evidence-based reading and writing and (2) math required sections on SAT. The total SAT score will be the sum of required section scores listed in Table D. The highest possible SAT score is 1600. If a student takes the optional Essay test, he or she will receive a separate score.

Table D: SAT Test Sections

SAT Sections	Number of Questions	Time Limit	Content Covered
Reading	52	65 minutes	Reading and vocabulary context
Writing	44	35 minutes	Grammar and usage
Math (no calculator)	20	25 minutes	Number and operations; algebra and functions; Geometry; data analysis; and probability
Math (calculator allowed)	38	55 minutes	Number and operations; algebra and functions; Geometry; data analysis; and probability
Essay (optional)	1 prompt	50 minutes	Writing skills

ACT

ACT, a non-profit organization, administers the ACT. The ACT assesses a student's high school academic performance. Correctly answered ACT questions are worth one point and without a penalty for incorrect answers on multiple choice parts. A student's score will not decrease for wrong answers. Students receive a composite ACT score that is the average score from the four required sections shown in Table E. The composite score will be on a scale from 1 to 36. If a student takes the optional Writing test, he or she will receive a separate score.

Table E: ACT Test Sections

ACT Sections	Number of Questions	Time Limit	Covered Content
English	75	45 minutes	Grammar & usage, punctuation, sentence structure
Math	60	60 minutes	Pre-algebra, Algebra I, Algebra 2, Geometry, Trigonometry
Reading	40	35 minutes	Reading comprehension (stated/implied)
Science Reasoning	40	35 minutes	Interpretation, analysis, evaluation, reasoning, and problem solving
Writing (optional)	1 prompt	40 minutes	Writing skills

Which Test to Take (Both the SAT and ACT)

Scholars should plan to take *both* these test before their senior year of high school. Most scholars take these tests the spring of their junior year and/or fall of their senior year. In fact, I recommend taking them both twice, as early as your sophomore year to see which test you naturally test the best on. Based on your performance on the SAT and ACT, I recommend you take a prep course for the test you perform the best on and then retake that test. I have seen scholars significantly increase their test scores when they take this approach.

Differences between the SAT and ACT

While the SAT and ACT both measure high school performance, there are numerous differences in these tests. Table F shows the differences in SAT and ACT cost, test duration, score range, and average test scores. Also, students now have the option to pay extra to get their actual test questions and answers sent to them. I highly recommend getting paying a little extra to get the real test questions and answers. Getting the actual test questions and answers will help students understand their testing strengths and weaknesses as the work on preparing before retaking the test.

Table F: SAT and ACT Test Information

Test	Cost	Test Q&A Score	Test Duration	Score Range	Average Test Score
SAT	$47.50 ($60 with the optional Essay)	$18	3 hrs (+ 50 min for optional Essay)	400 to 1600	1060
ACT	$46 ($62.50 with optional Writing)	$13	2 hrs 55 min (+ 40 min for optional Writing)	1 to 36	21

How to Register

Scholars can get SAT and ACT registration materials from their school guidance counselor, by mail or online. By registering online, the student can also pay by credit card. Below are the websites to register:

- To register for the SAT, visit the College Board site at: https://www.collegeboard.org
- To register for the ACT, visit the ACT site at: https://www.act.org.

Test dates and testing locations will be available on the websites. In many cases, there will be numerous testing locations to pick from that may be located near you. Some local high schools are used at test sites. Both SAT and ACT registration deadlines fall approximately five weeks before each test date. The scholar will need to set up an online account with a valid email address and specify a username and password. The online site will require students to provide information such as:

- Address
- Phone number
- Email address
- Parent's contact information
- High school information
- College major and career interests
- Colleges/organization code to send SAT/ACT scores

- Photo of test taker (in an acceptable format on the website) – the photo must be clear and no one else can be in the photo with the test taker

Test Fees

Generally, there are fees associated with taking the SAT and ACT Test. The SAT and ACT registration fee is about $46-48 (without essay or writing fees). These fees could increase if additional services are requested. Check the SAT and ACT websites for updated fee information. Some fees might include:

- Registration Fee – This covers one test date.
- Essay or Writing Fee – Covers the cost of the essay or writing part of the test.
- Subject Test Fee – Cost for each subject test fee.
- Change Test Fee – Cost to change the test center or test date.
- Late Registration Fee – Cost to register after the regular deadline but before the late registration deadline.
- Report Score Fee – Additional score report fee (outside of the number of free score reports provided with the registration fee).
- Test questions and answers – Cost to get a copy of your test questions and answers.

- Rush Score Fee – Cost to request a rush service to have score reports sent to colleges within two to four business days.

Some scholars may be eligible for an SAT fee waiver, where they can send as many free test score reports as they would like. To find out if a scholar is eligible, a school counselor or representative of an authorized community-based organization can help a student get a fee waiver. Proof of eligibility, such as tax records may be required.

Sending Test Score Reports

The scholar's SAT and/or ACT score reports are sent to the scholar's high school. Some scholars can specify what colleges and/or scholarship organizations to receive their test scores, during the application process, by selecting the appropriate codes online. Scholars can also send test reports to colleges and other organizations after they take the test.

For the SAT, a scholar can send up to four free test score reports to colleges up to nine days after taking the test. For the ACT, a scholar can send up to four free test score reports to colleges before taking the ACT and up to nine days after taking the SAT. After that, there is a fee (about $12 for each SAT test report and $13 for an ACT test report) to send each test score report. Also, for athletes, the NCAA requires scholars who seek eligibility to send test scores.

How to Prepare

Scholars can develop techniques and strategies to better prepare for the SAT and/or ACT, get accepted into competitive colleges, or earn higher test scores. I recommend that students take the SAT or ACT at least one time before paying for a prep course. Some organizations offer prep courses that conclude before the specific test dates. The most effective prep courses help the scholar prepare to take the test and improve their knowledge of the subject matter.

After completing a prep course, I recommend taking the SAT or ACT soon after. Depending on the scholar's learning style and financial situation, there are various types of preparatory programs that can be personalized to assist scholars by building on the scholar's strengths and improve the weaknesses. If a scholar has taken the SAT or ACT previously and paid to get the actual questions and answers from the test, the scholar should leverage this information to prepare before the next test. There are a variety of prep programs to choose from: traditional classroom, online, mobile apps, or blended approaches.

Organizations may offer paid and free resources such as practice tests, one-on-one, academic tutoring, and in-home prep assistance for the SAT and ACT. Look for programs that offer a self-paced option. Many students have busy schedules with school, jobs, extra-curricular activities and more. Flexibility will be important. Consider how your scholar learns best and your financial situation as you determine the best prep approach to take. For example, according to Reviews.com, the best 4 out of 37 prep courses listed in Table G.

Table G: SAT and ACT Prep Courses

Prep Resource	Type	Benefit	Cost
Kaplan	SAT/ACT	Most practice tests	$299 and up
The Princeton Review	SAT/ACT	Best one-on-one interaction	$299 and up
Khan Academy	SAT (only)	Best *free* SAT prep	Free
ACT Prep Online	ACT (only)	Most engaging ACT prep (fun)	$40 and up

Conduct online research to develop a complete list of available prep courses, practice tests, and other programs. Review the details of each program to understand which programs and courses reinforce the scholar's knowledge the best. To get you started, here are some prep websites and resources:

- Review.com - http://www.reviews.com/act-sat-test-prep-courses
- Kaplan - https://www.kaptest.com
- Khan Academy - https://www.khanacademy.org
- Princeton Review - https://www.princetonreview.com
- ACT Online Prep - https://www.act.org
- Kent Prep - https://kentprep.com
- PrepScholar - https://prepscholar.com/sat/s/
- Study Point - https://www.studypoint.com
- Test-guide - https://www.test-guide.com

PSAT

The Preliminary SAT (PSAT) is administered to mostly high school sophomores and juniors every year in October to provide scholars with practice for taking the SAT and ACT. The PSAT is a 2 hour, 45-minute multiple choice test. The PSAT is typically paid for by schools and students are registered through their high schools. The PSAT is very similar to the SAT, except the PSAT is 15 minutes shorter. Both the SAT and PSAT have a Math and Evidence-based Reading & Writing section. Prepping for the SAT is similar to prepping for the PSAT.

Although PSAT does not count toward qualifying for college admissions, the PSAT is used to identify and award national merit scholarships. Some students win a scholarship of $2,500 or more. Even if a scholar takes the PSAT and does not qualify for a national merit scholarship, this test can also help them become more familiar with the SAT format and to get an idea of how they might perform on the SAT.

Taking the SAT and ACT does not have to be onerous or stressful. Not everyone takes tests, well but that's even more reason to be deliberate and strategic in your actions. Ideally, plan on taking both the SAT and ACT to determine which test you naturally score the best on, then focus your efforts on approving your test score for that test. Also, plan on retaking one of the two tests more than once. Taking either the SAT or ACT test more than once could serve you well.

Some colleges use a super-scoring to determine the applications best test scores on each section from multiple tests administered to determine admissions acceptance. For example, if you take the ACT and score a 21 on the Math section and a 19 on the English section the first time, and when you retake the ACT, you score a 19 on the Math section and a 22 on the English section. The college might take the 21

Math score from your first ACT and the 22 English score from your second test.

Also, plan to do some prep work and/or take a prep course to improve your score. Then, retake the test soon after completing the prep course. This could be a small price to pay to get into the college of your choice and/or received potentially thousands of dollars in scholarship and financial aid funding. Also, there are free SAT and ACT prep courses and apps. Do a little research to find the best prep approach for you based on what you can afford.

If you are a senior and may not have time to retake the SAT or ACT multiple times, so take a prep course, then take the SAT/ACT test before applying to college anyway. Focus on matching your high school performance and test scores with colleges. Colleges are interested in more than just your SAT/ACT score. In fact, some colleges are making these tests optional, and some colleges only use SAT or ACT scores to determine for financial aid purposes. Do not assume that a low score on the SAT or ACT will keep you are high, you may have great odds.

STRATEGY 7: RESEARCH AND VISIT COLLEGES

"Research is creating new knowledge." Neil Armstrong

Selecting a college is a critical aspect of college planning process. Since every individual is different, it is essential to assess your background, interests, goals, career aspirations, and personality. When considering your college options and college majors, make your decision based on your plan.

Research

Some scholars begin researching colleges as early as middle school. If you in high school, move fast and start researching and narrowing down colleges you would like to attend. This search should start as early as your sophomore and junior year of high school. Every college and university has its own strengths and weaknesses. Therefore, try not to think about colleges as good or bad. Each college is different and your goal should be to try to find the best fit for you.

You can search by visiting: (1) school websites and hunting for information or (2) sites that have already done the legwork of compiling college information in one place. Students can search for colleges by location, major, tuition, and more. Search online to find sites that allow you to put in your college preferences to explore colleges. For example, the *Big Future-College Search, CollegeView.com, CollegeProwler.com, or Unigo.com* websites allow students to search from over 4,000 colleges from their website using an interactive college search guide.

Researching schools appears to be a daunting process, but if you spend a little time thinking about what is important to you, the research will pay off. The more you learn early on about different colleges, the more informed college selection choice you can make. Conduct research using online resources to obtain a wealth of information about colleges in a short period.

College Selection Factors

Narrow down your search by identifying the college selectin factors that you find. Table H depicts the *Sample College Selection Factors Level of Importance Spreadsheet* **(Template 4)** to help you rank selection factors that are important to you. Use the table to add selection factors that are important and fill in colleges at the top that you wish to research. Rank the factors that are important to you and complete the table by researching each college you have an interest. Then, compare and contrast the colleges that align with your top selection factors. Add as many colleges as you desire to the list to research.

Table H: Sample College Selection Factors Level of Importance

Level of Importance	Selection Factors	College A	College B	College C
	Location of college			
	Distance from home			
	College size			
	Class size			
	City or neighborhood			
	Campus culture			
	Campus environment			
	Housing options near campus			
	Program of study			
	Accreditations			
	Annual cost to attend			
	Financial aid options			
	Campus Transportation			
	Extracurricular activities			
	Religious affiliation			
	Food/Meal options			

Consider conducting online research to see how colleges and universities may rank nationally. For example, the U.S. News provides numerical rankings and lists of colleges nationwide to assist students with narrowing down their college search. Scholars can find the best college choice for them by exploring National Universities, Liberal Arts Colleges, and A-Plus Schools for B Students.

Once you conduct research and narrow down your college selections, you will need to understand the college admission requirements of your top college selections. Focus your valuable time and efforts on colleges you have an interest in attending and those you have the highest chance of being accepted. College admission officials will review your application package to admissions requirements to make an admissions decision. Research college admission requirements as you have narrowed down colleges based on your selection factors. At any rate, researching college admission requirements will be necessary to ensure that you meet the college's admission eligibility requirements.

College Admission Requirements

Complete the *College Requirement Spreadsheet* (**Template 5**) for your top 5-10 top college interests. As shown in the Sample College Requirement Spreadsheet, a scholar can use this spreadsheet to capture information about each college researched.

COLLEGE REQUIREMENTS SPREADSHEET													
COLLEGE NAME	LOCATION	COLLEGE TOUR	YEARLY TUITION/ROOM & BOARD COST	APPLICATION (ONLINE OR MAIL)	APPLICATION FEE	EARLY ADMISSION DATE	DEADLINE TO APPLY	GPA	SAT SCORE	ACT SCORE	ESSAY (Y/N)	LETTERS OF RECOMMENDATION (Y/N)	WEBSITE
Sample University	City, State	Yes	$ 36,660	Online	$ 35	10/30/20XX	3/1/20XX	3.3	1100	22	Y, 250-500 words	Y, 1	www.college.edu
Name	City, State												

The spreadsheet should capture information such as:

- College Name
- Location
- College visit/tour
- Annual tuition/expenses
- Apply (paper or electronic)
- Admission/Early admission deadline
- Application fee
- GPA (average or minimum)
- SAT requirement
- ACT requirement
- Essay required (yes or no)
- Essay word count requirement (#)
- Letters of recommendation (#)

69

- Admissions point of contact

- Type of scholarships available

- Website link

- Date application submitted

- Acceptance decision

- Additional information/notes

After completing the *College Requirement Spreadsheet,* you can better determine which college(s) you may want to apply to. You should narrow down the number of colleges you want to apply that offers you the best probability of getting accepted, the cost of attending, the location, and other factors. Having this information on each school listed in one spreadsheet should make it easy for you to pay attention to key deadlines and actions you must take to meet those deadlines. If you are entering your senior year of high school, consider applying early in the fall to get an early admissions decision. If so, begin writing essays and getting letters of recommendations in the summer and early fall of your senior year.

College Visits and Tours

Visiting and touring colleges is a great way to compare colleges and campuses to narrow down your college search. Touring colleges is also a great way for homeschooled scholars and others to ask specific questions about requirements and eligibility. You can learn quite a bit just by traveling to colleges of interest to learn more about the college environment, campus life, professionalism of campus staff, safety and security, proximity to activities, and more. Try to get a feel for whether or not the campus fits with your personality and whether you fit in that college's environment. Plan to visit and tour colleges early as possible, but no later than the spring of your junior year.

Schedule college visits during school breaks or on family vacations. You can also take a special trip to visit colleges. If you would like a guided college tour, call ahead to the college admissions office to schedule a tour. If possible, consider visiting during the weekday when college classes are taking place. Visiting while college is in session will give you a great chance to evaluate the campus atmosphere. Possibly ask to sit in on a class to check out the scenery or assess the class size. Do not waste valuable tour time asking questions that you have already researched. Develop a list of questions before visiting each college that you want to know more about. Also, check out websites that offer virtual college campus tours, like **www.ecampustours.com**. This website allows students to go on a virtual 360° x 360° tour for thousands of colleges.

College Fairs

In addition to college tours, attend college fairs to learn more about colleges and their programs. At college fairs, representatives from multiple colleges gather to provide high school students with information about their college. Colleges hold fairs at high schools, local libraries, community centers, or virtually online. College representatives generally sit or stand at booths or tables and pass out college materials to students. These representatives can answer questions about college admissions requirements and general questions about their college. College WeekLive is an example of a free virtual college fair website where students can interact with hundreds of college representatives around the world. Scholars can attend virtual college fairs online. Virtual college fairs offer the same benefits of attending a fair in person. Students can visit virtual booths to get more information about colleges.

STRATEGY 8: APPLY TO COLLEGES

"Rejection is an opportunity for your selection." Bernard Branson

The culmination of your high school years, academic performance, extracurricular activities, and leadership shape the story you tell about yourself through your college application. All of your hard work, dedication, commitment, and follow-through will finally reveal the fruits of your labor now that you are applying to colleges. The question is how you will look on paper? When your application package arrives at college admissions offices, and others make decisions about your acceptance into their college, what will your college application say? Will your college application package represent you well? Will it differentiate you from others?

When to Apply to Colleges

The best time to apply to colleges is early in the fall of your senior year. Generally, you should apply in the September/October timeframe. Find out if the college has a deadline for an early admissions decision. In this chapter, practical strategies will be shared with you that could differentiate you from other applicants. As shown in the figure, rising high school seniors should start the college application process as early as the summer before their senior year.

College Application Process

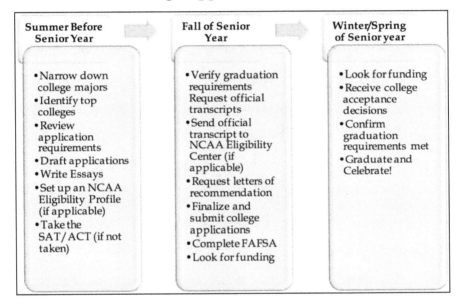

Summer Before Senior Year	Fall of Senior Year	Winter/Spring of Senior year
• Narrow down college majors • Identify top colleges • Review application requirements • Draft applications • Write Essays • Set up an NCAA Eligibility Profile (if applicable) • Take the SAT/ACT (if not taken)	• Verify graduation requirements Request official transcripts • Send official transcript to NCAA Eligibility Center (if applicable) • Request letters of recommendation • Finalize and submit college applications • Complete FAFSA • Look for funding	• Look for funding • Receive college acceptance decisions • Confirm graduation requirements met • Graduate and Celebrate!

College Admissions Requirements

Your *College Admissions Requirements Spreadsheet* will serve as an essential tool as you begin your college application journey since you used this to gather application and eligibility information about your top selected colleges. If necessary, take time to refresh this spreadsheet with updated college information before continuing. Add or delete colleges based on your evolving college interests.

Then, re-prioritize the colleges on the spreadsheet based on the deadline to complete a college application. Based on your research, a college may require that you apply on paper or electronically. Some colleges will give you an option. If given a choice, consider submitting your application electronically online. Applying online has some advantages. You may be able get confirmation that your college application was received. You may also track your college application as it progresses through the decision process. The college application package contains five main parts including: (1) the college application, (2) official high school transcripts, (3) essay(s), (4) letters of recommendation, and (5) test scores.

College Applications

Visit the college's website to obtain the most current version of their college application. The college application may be downloaded or you may have to create an account online to complete the application. Scholars should start the college application process about six weeks before submitting. Allow two to three weeks to complete the application and a month to gather other required documents (transcripts, letters of recommendations, and essays). Your completed *Scholar Profile* can serve as a beneficial resource during this process. Use your Scholar Profile to fill in relevant content on your application. Do not skip steps or fail to submit required information.

Print two copies of the college application. Use the first copy to complete a rough draft of the application before you submit a final clean version. Double check to make sure there are no typos or grammatical errors. Consider having a trusted adult review your entire package before mailing it.

- Paper Application: If you must submit a paper copy of the college application consider the following tips:
  o Type the application (unless the college requests explicitly that a hand-written application). Consider using a trial version of Adobe to convert the downloadable college application for typing.
  o Make a copy of the entire college application package for your records before putting in the mail.
  o Save and reuse as many documents as much as you can electronically.
  o Make sure you use the correct mailing **address** to mail the college application package.
  o Ensure that the entire package (including transcripts) are mailed and postmarked before the application deadline.

o Send the college application package in a weather-proof envelope and mail it with a (1) delivery confirmation and (2) signature required. Do this even if you have to pay extra. Nothing is worse than the university stating they never received your package. Without delivery receipt confirmation or tracking, you will be at a disadvantage proving otherwise. Tracking your application package will also give you confidence that your package was received on time and by the deadline.

- Electronic Application: If you submit an electronic college application consider the following tips:
  o Set-up an online account and get comfortable navigating around.
  o Do not wait until the application deadline is near to get familiar with the system.
  o Document and keep track of your username and passwords for each college account.
  o Save a copy of the entire college application package for your records before submitting it.
  o Save and reuse as many documents as much as you can electronically.

- Submit your entire package (including transcripts) *before* the application deadline. Keep in mind that large submission volumes may lead to system failures if you wait until the deadline.
- Save a copy of the delivery or submission confirmation. Sometimes the submission confirmation contains a time and date stamp. Nothing is worse than a lost package that no one can track.
- As you apply to colleges, document and track the which colleges you applied to, the date you applied, and whether you applied on paper or electronically.

The Common Application

Completing your college application is a critical step in the college planning process. Take advantage of the resources available to streamline the process like the Common Application (App) at www.commonapp.org. The Common App is a non-profit member organization that allows students can submit one college applications to over 750 colleges. More than one million first-time and transfer applicants submit college applications using the Common App. While not required, scholars can research and apply to multiple colleges through one website. The scholar's information is stored on the site and reused when applying for multiple colleges on the site. This could save the time and effort.

Applicants can search which colleges participate in the Common App's program. The Common App opens on August 1st of each year. Applicants can open an account on the commonapp.org website (click on "Get Started") at any time. Information provided can be transferred into the new app when it opens. The best time for an applicant to start the Common App is in the summer of your senior year. Applicants can use the Common App for free, and roughly 45% of participating schools do not charge an application fee. If a participating school requires an application fee, the applicant pays the application fee when they submit the application to the college.

Official Transcripts

Providing an official transcript is a critical part of the college admission decision process. Official high school transcripts are formal copies of a student's official academic grades and courses from grades 9-12. When scholars began taking high school courses, high school officials calculate official transcript grades from final semester or quarter grades and course credits received. In fact, some scholars start taking high school courses as early as middle school; therefore, it is critical that you make the best grades possible in all high school courses. Most colleges require homeschooled students to take specific courses and to submit a high school transcript. Some colleges offer templates to help homeschooled students document courses and to convert grades into a calculated GPA. Templates may also be available online.

Keep in mind that if you apply to colleges in the fall of your senior year, your official transcripts will have only your grades from your freshman through your junior year. These official transcripts usually contain unique markings that signify the copies are authentic. Most colleges will require official high school transcripts be sent directly from your high school. Most colleges will not accept transcripts provided by students or transcripts that have been opened unless a college provides specific instructions. Parental permission may be required before a scholar can even request a transcript at their high school. Make sure you understand your high school's transcript request process and follow it precisely.

Don't wait until the last minute to request transcripts. In fact, once you have a list of colleges you plan on applying to, request to have your official high school transcripts sent to all your colleges at one time. This will ensure that your official transcripts will be sent on time or ahead of time. Based on my experience, college admission officials wait to make acceptance decisions until they receive the official high school transcripts. Most high schools will either mail or email your official transcripts to colleges. Double check with the colleges to verify they receive your high school transcripts by the deadline. If the college has not received your transcript, promptly follow-up with your high school.

Essays

Some college applications may require an essay. Colleges use the essay to learn more about your academic performance (grades) that standardized test scores cannot. Your essay provides college admission officials more insight into who you are as a person. Use your essay as an opportunity to showcase yourself and share information not conveyed previously on your application.

You may be instructed to write on a particular topic or given the freedom to choose a specific topic or theme. Follow the essay instructions by such as the specified minimum or maximum word or character count. If you draft your essay in Microsoft Word, select the text you want to count. Then, go to "Tools" and then "Word Count" to find out your essay's word count or character count. If the college provides a template or format, please use it and do not deviate from it.

Also, whether essay instructions specify it or not, always type your essay. Individual handwriting may be difficult to read.

If you use the Common App to apply to colleges, check the essay requirements for participating colleges through the Common App site. When applicants log in to the Common App's website, applicants can see the requirements. There may be approximately seven essay prompts with a 250-word count minimum and a 650-word count maximum. Review the Common App's website for current information and changes.

Useful Essay Writing Tips:

- BE YOURSELF. Make sure your essay reflects who you are.

- Start early. Recommend the summer before your senior year.

- Address the essay topic or answer the question asked.

- Stick to the required word count minimum or maximum. Use your word processing software to confirm your word count.

- Brainstorm to generate ideas. Be creative.

- Consider developing a brief outline to organize your thoughts.

- Develop your first draft and make sure your essay has three parts: (1) an introduction, (2) a body, and (3) a conclusion.

- Keep your topic narrow and focused. Don't cover too many topics.

- Show your knowledge about the college with a few relevant facts or statistics.

- Avoid clichés. Don't rely on words or ideas others have previously used.

- Get feedback from someone who writes well (a parent or teacher). Have them edit your essay.

- Proofread and make corrections. Plan to write several drafts.

Letters of Recommendations

College applications may instruct you to submit letters of recommendations. Strong letters of recommendation from trusted references can help differentiate you from other applicants. Read each of your college's application instructions to ensure you know how many letters of recommendations are needed, what types of letters of recommendations, and how they would like the letters of recommendations delivered. Colleges may specify that they would like letters of recommendation on a particular subject or from a specific type of teacher, guidance counselor or other professional.

Useful Letter of Recommendation Strategies

- Request letters of recommendations (early in your senior school year) from individuals who you believe would provide you with a good reference and provide any specific instructions the college may require.

- Start identifying teachers from grades 9-11 who may be willing.

- Keep a list of teachers who might be willing to write about you.

- Do not wait until the last minute to ask.

- Give references plenty of time and notice to write your letter of recommendation.

- Provide your references a deadline at least two weeks before your deadline. This deadline should be earlier than your official application deadline to give you a buffer. Provide those who will write your letter your updated *Scholar Profile* to help them write more accurately about you as a person. If it will save them time or you have a tight deadline.

- Offer to provide them a draft a letter of recommendation and have them customize the letter. This might be an appealing proposition for busy professionals and this might help you to get your letter of recommendation back sooner.

- Don't forget to thank everyone who provided you letters of recommendations.

Test Scores

Consider that most colleges require official test scores. Students typically submit SAT or ACT scores as part of the college application process. Most students send test scores to colleges before or after the SAT or ACT date. Before taking the SAT and ACT, have a list of colleges you wish to send your test score reports to. Send your SAT or ACT scores to colleges to which you plan to apply. You will likely have to log in to the SAT and/or ACT website and provide the college's specific code as you request to send your test scores.

STRATEGY 9: NAVIGATE THE FUNDING PROCESS

"An investment in knowledge pays the best interest." Benjamin Franklin

Navigating the process to find funding to pay for college expenses can be challenging. Understanding how to finding funding can be one of the most critical parts of the college admissions process. Tuition and fees can be expensive and unless parents and or scholars have the financial resources and economic means, paying for college might be difficult. Parents and scholars are responsible for paying for college. Scholars may incur numerous expenses in college. Some expenses may include:

- Tuition and fees: The price colleges charge for students to take classes and receive course instructions.

- Room and Board: The cost of living expenses for housing and meals to students.

- Books and supplies: The cost of textbooks, notebooks, paper, course materials, calculators, and computer supplies, software resources, and more.

- Personal expenses: The cost of living including laundry, meals, clothes, cell phone, entertainment, and medical experiences.

- Transportation: The cost to commute to and from campus, trips home, or to work.

From 2005-2015, the U.S. Department of Education, National Center for Education Statistics (2016) estimated the average cost of undergraduate tuition, room and board, and other fees at public institutions increased by 33 percent. For the 2014-2015 academic year, the average cost of college education, for a full-time student attending a four-year public institution was $16,188, $41,970 at private nonprofit institutions, and $23,372 at private for-profit institutions.

College costs and expenses vary from college to college. Public institutions may be more economical than some private institutions. Your earlier research will help you the understand the differences in cost. The cost to attend college continues to rise each academic year, and it is increasingly important to plan early and work strategically to offset the cost of college.

There are different ways to fund the cost of college. Students may likely leverage more than on one funding source to meet their financial needs.

Funding Sources

- **Out of pocket**: Some families have the income and savings to pay for college out of pocket without the need for additional funding.

- **College savings plans**: Many states have education specific and other investment plans to help parents and students save money with tax advantages.

- **Retirement plans:** Some parents set up a Roth IRA to pay for college expenses because parents may be able to withdraw principal funds that are tax-free and penalty-free at any time and for any reason.

- **Scholarships:** Money or a form of "gift aid" from private, non-profit, or community organizations that scholars do not have repay. Scholarships are not the same as financial aid.

- **Financial aid:** Financial aid is money to help pay for college. Aid generally comes from various sources (1) the U. S. federal government, (2) the state or local government where you live, (3) college you seek to attend, and (3) private, nonprofit, or community organizations.

Federal Financial Aid

Federal financial aid is a significant source of college funding. The main types of financial aid include: grants, loans, and work study.

- Grants: Financial aid that does not have to refunded or paid (unless you withdraw from college and owe a repaid).

- Loans: Money borrowed for college that must be repaid with interest. Borrow only what you need.

- Work Study: A program where you can earn money to help pay for college.

Do not wait until the spring of your senior year to begin looking for additional funding. Some funding sources have deadlines and other funding entities award money on a first come first serve basis. It is never too early to start thinking about funds for college. If you find great sources of funding, save them and book mark them so that you can reference these sources at the right time. As you run across organizations, websites, or other sources don't lose sight of them, store them away for future use. During your junior year and early senior year, you should be preparing to apply to colleges and to focus more on looking for funding.

Free Application for Federal Student Aid

In 2018, the U.S. Department of Education awarded more than $120 billion each year in financial aid to over 13 million students. Scholars who seek federal financial aid funding must begin by completing a Free Application for Federal Student Aid (FAFSA). Colleges use the FAFSA to determine a scholar's eligibility for all financial aid. Submitting the FAFSA is free and most scholars apply online (www.fafsa.gov) because it is fast, easy, and accurate.

Complete the FAFSA during the fall of your senior year of high school. Provide accurate and complete information. Submitting your application online is secure, and your personal information will be safeguarded. There are organizations that offer to help you complete your FAFSA by charging you a fee, but you do not need to pay for their services because you can complete the application yourself.

You will answer a series of questions. Preview the FAFSA questions online on the worksheet at: https://studentaid.ed.gov/sa/sites/default/files/2017-18-fafsa-worksheet.pdf. The questions on the worksheet are listed in the same order they appear with the online application. Some questions may be skipped based on how you answered previous questions. You will also need to provide or select the federal school codes for all the colleges where you apply.

Prepare in advance by gathering up documents such as prior-year federal income tax returns, W-2 forms, current bank statements, and records of benefits from state/federal agencies. Both students and their parents will need to create a Federal Student Aid (FSA) ID to sign electronically. Once you complete your FAFSA, you will receive a Student Aid Report (SAR) that specifies your Expected Family Contribution (EFC). The EFC does not describe the amount of money you and your family must pay. Rather, the EFC is an index used by colleges to calculate the amount of financial aid you may qualify to receive.

Some people do not complete the FAFSA because they: (1) assume they do not qualify for federal aid, (2) believe the process is complicated, or (3) find the process difficult to understand. Do not assume that you do are not eligible for financial aid. However, if you fail to complete the FAFSA, you will be ineligible to receive federal financial aid. Additionally, in some states, you will still need to complete the FAFSA to be considered for state financial aid. Also, colleges and some private entity scholarship programs used FAFSA data to determine eligibility for some scholarships.

91

Most scholars complete their first FAFSA during their senior year of high school. Scholars will be required to complete a new FAFSA each year he or she attends college. Based on the information submitted, federal financial aid is calculated using a formula mandated by Congress. The formula factors in your financial condition. Plan to complete a FAFSA each year even if you are not seeking federal financial aid, because states and colleges also will also use FAFSA data to determine eligibility.

Award Letter

The colleges you applied to will receive your FAFSA information. The college will use that information to determine the amount and the types of aid you may qualify for and send you an award letter. The award letter will describe your estimated cost of attendance and your total financial aid package that may include: scholarships, grants, loans, and/or work-study.

Once you receive your award letter, it will be important to make sure you understand the information contained in the award letter and that you respond back to the college before the deadline specified in your award letter. If you do not respond back by the deadline, you may lose your financial aid. Read and review your award letter carefully to make sure you understand your financial aid options, terms, and conditions before you accept any or all of the aid offered. In some cases, you might be instructed to provide additional paperwork or documentation. If multiple colleges accept you, review all award letters and compare your financial aid award options and make the best decision for you. Table I depicts a **Sample College Award Letter** that gives you an idea of the types of financial aid a scholar may receive.

After reviewing your award letter consider that the award does not cover all your expenses and that you may still have out-of-pocket costs. You may grow concerned if your family contributions are not enough to cover the additional costs. Stay encouraged! There are many other options to consider to help offset the expenses for you to attend your desired costs. Because there are numerous ways to offset the cost of college, you should apply for financial aid early because you want to leave yourself time to look for other funding. Conduct more research to find other funding sources such as private scholarships and employee tuition benefits.

Table I: Sample College Award Letter

Sample College Award Letter	
Costs in 20XX-20XX	**Costs/Year**
Estimated cost of attendance for full-time enrollment	$35,000
Tuition and fees	$21,000
Housing and meals (on-campus resident)	$10,000
Books and supplies	$2,000
Transportation	$1,000
Other educational costs	$1,000
Grants and Scholarships to Pay for College	**Costs/Year**
Total Grants and Scholarships (no repayment required)	$15,000
Grants from the college	$7,500
Federal Pell Grant	$3,500
Grants from the state	$1,000
Transportation	$1,200
Other scholarship funds	$1,800
What You Will Pay for 20XX-20XX	**Costs/Year**
Net Costs (Cost of attendance minus total grants and scholarships)	$20,000
Options to Pay Net Costs	
Work Options	**Costs/Year**
Work-Study (Federal, state, or institutional)	$5,000
Loan Options (recommended amounts)	**Costs/Year**
Federal Perkins Loan	$5,500
Federal Direct Subsidized Loan	$3,500
Federal Direct Unsubsidized Loan	$2,000
Parent Plus Loan (if eligible)	Varies
Other Options	**Costs/Year**
Family contribution (As calculated by the college based on reported FAFSA information)	$4,000
Payment plan offered by the college	TBD
Parent or Graduate PLUS Loan	TBD
Military and/or other National Service Benefits	TBD
Non-Federal private education loans	TBD
Source: Financial Aid Shopping Sheet, U.S. Department of Education College Affordability and Transparency Center, https://www2.ed.gov/policy/highered/guid/aid-offer/index.html	

Non-Federal Aid

Over 400 colleges, professional schools, and scholarship programs use the CSS Profile (https://cssprofile.collegeboard.org) to award non-federal aid. The CSS Profile is an online application that collects information that colleges use to offer scholarship and grant awards to students. Participating colleges can evaluate a student's financial need and provide financial assistance. If the student has a SAT College Board account, the same credentials can be used to sign in to the CSS Profile account. The initial application fee is $25 (check the website for updated fee costs). Additional reports are $16 each.

Scholarships

Scholarships are gifts or funds that can help offset college expenses that scholars do not have to repay. There are thousands of scholarships awarded annually. Each year, many students receive scholarship funds to offset college expenses, and others receive enough money to cover all of their college expenses. Obtaining scholarship funds requires diligence and research. There are various types of scholarships such as: academic, athletic, or military service related. Moreover, there is an abundance of scholarships awarded each year that are not athletic or merit-based.

Scholarships are offered based on a variety of topics, interests, or criteria including:

- Financial need
- High school attended
- Ethnicity
- Gender
- College scholarships
- College major or interest
- Civic or community service
- Employment tuition programs
- Federal programs
- States and counties
- Individuals
- Organizations
- Interests, hobbies, skills
- Religion
- Military service

Military Service Scholarships

Military services such as the U.S. Navy, Army, and Air Force offer numerous scholarships for military service member veterans, dependents of veterans, and students. In addition, there are also high school students can apply for

Reserve Officer Training Corps (ROTC) competitive merit-based scholarships. These services all offer scholarships to help scholars reduce college education financial burden. In many cases, these ROTC programs will collaborate with specific colleges. These scholarships may provide full-tuition scholarships to additional funding for room and board, books and fees, and a stipend. Scholarship recipients may be commissioned as officers and required to serve in the military after college graduation. Also, some scholarships are two-year, three-year, and four-year scholarships. The application requirements, deadlines, and available funding awards may vary for each type of scholarship. Visit military service and individual college websites for specific details on veteran, dependent, and ROTC programs.

- Air Force ROTC: https://www.afrotc.com/scholarships
- Army ROTC: https://www.goarmy.com/rotc/scholarships.html
- Naval ROTC: http://www.nrotc.navy.mil/scholarships.html

Researching Scholarship

If you have a 3.0 GPA, you have a high probability of finding scholarship funds. In fact, scholars with a 3.0 GPA should NOT have to pay for college out-of-pocket. Visit with your high school guidance counselors, family, friends, and employers to see if they have good scholarship sources or contacts. Local community scholarships are great ways to get funding because many students do not know about these opportunities and there may only be a few applicants for each scholarship. Scholarship funding will not just fall into your lap. You must be willing to search for scholarship opportunities. The best way to search and apply for scholarships is to develop a plan.

At the same time, the Internet is a great way to begin a scholarship search. There are hundreds of search sites on the web. Some websites may require you to set up an account and provide personal information to establish a profile before you can search for scholarships. Be aware of submitting your personal formation because not all sites are legitimate. Some legitimate sites are:

- Fastweb: www.fastweb.com
- College Board: www.bigfuture.collegeboard.org
- College Scholarships: www.collegescholarships.com
- Scholarship.com: www.Scholarships.com
- U.S. Department of Labor: www.careerinfonet.org/scholarshipsearch
- Scholly: www.myscholly.com

Applying for Scholarship

The best way to receive a scholarship award is to apply for scholarships. Apply for all potential scholarships to increase your chances of success. Scholarship application requirements and instructions may vary so pay attention to the details. Some scholarships may require you to provide additional information such as items listed below:

- Essays
- Letters of recommendation
- Examples of work experience
- Photograph(s)
- SAT/ACT Scores
- Transcripts
- Telephone or in-person interviews
- College acceptance letters
- FAFSA information

As you apply for scholarships, get organized and consider these helpful tips:

- Develop a checklist for all required documents and actions you must take for each application.
- Complete a draft of your application on paper before developing a final application.

- Follow all directions on the application.
- If possible, type all applications (unless otherwise specified on the application).
- Attach all required additional information to the application. Consider attaching a copy of your *Scholar Profile* to set yourself apart from the competition.
- Review your application for completeness, and typos.
- Have someone review your application.
- Save a copy of all applications before submitting them.
- Submit your application before the deadline.
- Use a tracking tool to document submitted scholarship application information in one place such as this *Sample Scholarship Tracking Spreadsheet* (**Template 6**).

Sample Scholarship Tracking Spreadsheet

SCHOLARSHIP TRACKING SPREADSHEET										
No	Scholarship	Amount	Qualifications	Website Link	Application Information	Deadline to Apply	Link to Application	ESSAY (Y/N)	LETTERS OF RECOMMENDATION (Y/N)	DATE APPLICATION SUBMITTED	DECISION
1	Name										
2	Name										

After applying for scholarships, you will likely receive correspondence from the scholarship sponsor to let you know if they selected you for the scholarship. You may receive notification by mail or email. If you receive scholarship funds, the sponsor may send the funds directly to you or the sponsor may send the funds directly to the college. Communicate with the college you plan to attend and share that you received outside scholarships because colleges must consider the additional scholarship funds in your financial aid package. In some cases, the college may adjust or reduce the amount of financial aid offered by the college based on scholarship amounts received.

STRATEGY 10: UNDERSTAND NCAA ELIGIBILITY

"The NCAA has its rules. It's our job to abide by them."
Ezekiel Elliott

The NCAA must deem high school student-athletes eligible to play and receive athletic aid. The NCAA is a member-driven organization focused on the well-being and success of college athletes. Over 1100 colleges and 110 Athletic Conferences are NCAA members. Nearly 500,000 athletes compete in 24 Division I, II, and III sports each year. NCAA members set recruiting and compliance rules and policies for college sports to benefit athletes. NCAA has a guide to assist with understanding eligibility requirements: http://www.ncaapublications.com/productdownloads/CB SA18.pdf.

Academic performance is just as, if not more important than athletic performance. Athletes cannot merely focus on sports performance to qualify to play collegiate sports or to receive an athletic scholarship. High school student-athletes must focus on academic achievements and meet standards to play collegiate sports. As early as middle school, student-athletes should understand athletic eligibility and scholarship requirements to ensure they meet and exceed expectations. If

102

you are a high school junior or senior and you are not familiar with athletic requirements to play collegiate sports in college, you should take immediate action to ensure you understand your eligibility.

Eligibility

Scholars who plan to play sports in college should be familiar with NCAA eligibility requirements for Division I, II, and III colleges. NCAA has specific eligibility requirements for Division I and II schools. Division III schools usually set their eligibility and academic standards. To be eligible to practice, compete, and receive an athletic scholarship in your first full-time enrollment year at Division I or Division II colleges, the college-bound student-athlete must meet all NCAA-approved academic and athletic requirements that include:

- Meet the 16 core course requirements specific to NCAA Division I or Division II.
- Meet GPA and SAT/ACT score requirements based on the Division I or Division II sliding scales.
- Complete Amateurism certificate.
- Graduate from high school.

NCAA Eligibility Center

Student-athletes who plan to play Division I or II sports in college, students must be registered and certified with the NCAA Eligibility Center (https://web3.ncaa.org/ecwr3/) to ensure they have met the academic and amateurism standards. Student-athletes should register with the NCAA Eligibility Center no later than the beginning of their sophomore year in high school to have sufficient time to make sure you are on track to graduate on time and to meet the NCAA's initial-eligibility standards. If you are planning to attend a Division III school, you do not need to register with the NCAA Eligibility Center.

To play Division I or II college sports, you should create either a Certification Account or a Profile Page:

- Certification Account(Division I or II): Create a Certification Account on the NCAA Eligibility Center site. There is an $80 fee (for U.S./Canada students) and $135 (or International students) (check the NCAA Eligibility website for updated fee amounts). Student-athletes will need to create a Certification Account to make official visits to Division I and II colleges or to sign a National Letter of Intent. For Certification Accounts, you may need to provide details about expenses or awards you receive or teams you have played on outside of the traditional high school season. This information is used by the Eligibility Center to certify your amateur status. After you complete your Certification Account, you can begin viewing your status notifications on your Dashboard under each sport you have selected.

- Profile Page (Division III): Create a Profile Page on the NCAA Eligibility Center site if you are considering playing at a Division III school or if you are undecided. You can change your mind and to upgrade to a Certification Account later. There is no charge to set up a Profile Page.

NCAA ID Number

When students set up an account, they will receive an NCAA ID that should be referenced for NCAA eligibility business or used during the recruiting process. To find your NCAA ID number, log in to your NCAA Eligibility Center account at eligibilitycenter.org. Your NCAA ID number is in the top-right corner, below your name.

Sliding Scale

NCAA uses a sliding scale approach to match a student-athlete's core-course GPA with SAT/ACT scores to determine NCAA eligibility. The sliding scale balances your GPA and test score. If you have a lower test score, you will need a higher GPA to be eligible. Conversely, if you have a low GPA, you will need a higher test score to qualify. There is a separate scale to meet Division I requirements and Division II requirements. Reference the most accurate sliding scales from the NCAA Eligibility Center site: http://www.ncaa.org/student-athletes/future/eligibility-center.

Core-Course Grade Point Average

Student-athletes must meet NCAA Eligibility academic and GPA requirements to play Division I and/or Division II sports as shown in Table J. NCAA has 16 core courses that high school athletes must pass to meet the NCAA's initial-eligibility standards (after first six semesters of high school) and final academic standards after graduating (end of senior year). Only NCAA-approved core courses will be used to calculate your core-course GPA. Visit the NCAA Eligibility Center site (http://www.ncaa.org/student-athletes/future/core-courses) for the most accurate list of NCAA-approved core courses and GPA requirements.

Table J: NCAA Division I and II GPA and Core Course Requirements

Eligibility Requirements	Minimum GPA	Core Course Requirements (16)
Division I	2.3	(4) years or English (3) years of math (Algebra I or higher) (2) years of natural/ physical science (2) years of social science (1) year of additional English, math, or natural/physical science (4) years of additional courses (any above area, foreign language or comparative religion/philosophy)
Division II	2.2	(3) years or English (2) years of math (Algebra I or higher) (2) years of natural/ physical science (2) years of social science (3) year of additional English, math, or natural/physical science (4) years of additional courses (any above area, foreign language or comparative religion/philosophy)

Your core-course GPA is calculated using the best 16 core courses that meet the subject-area requirements such as:

- English
- Math
- Natural/Physical Science
- Social Science
- Foreign Language

- Comparative Religion or Philosophy

The NCAA does not consider all courses as approved core courses such as:

- Music
- Physical Education
- Typing
- Art
- Personal Finance
- Welding
- Drivers Education
- Film Appreciation
- Photography

In addition, student-athletes must earn a minimum GPA of 2.3 to play Division I collegiate sports and a minimum GPA of 2.2 to play Division II collegiate sports. The NCAA calculates a student's GPA based on a 4.000 scale. Student athletes can calculate the core course GPA using the NCAA Division I or Division II Worksheet.

NCAA requires student-athletes who do not meet the minimum Division I requirements to "Redshirt" their first full-time collegiate enrollment year. These athletes may practice in the initial term and receive athletic aid during the initial year of full-time collegiate enrollment; however, they may not complete in sports during their first year of full-time enrollment.

Transcript

The NCAA Eligibility Center requires student-athletes to submit high school transcripts. Some high schools require students to complete a NCAA Eligibility Center Transcript Release Form. This form authorizes the high school to send an official transcript through grade 11 (first six-semesters) and/or final transcripts for students registered with the NCAA Eligibility Center. Faxed or emailed transcripts are not accepted. The fastest way to submit transcripts is by having your high school counselor use the direct upload approach on the High School portal, and your transcripts may be received the same day. If you mail your high school transcripts, it could take up to two to three business days before the college processes your transcript.

Sending SAT or ACT Scores

The NCAA requires Student-athletes to report their SAT or ACT scores to the NCAA Eligibility Center. Consider listing the NCAA Eligibility Center as an SAT or ACT score recipient (the code is "9999" for both the SAT and ACT) at the time of the exam registration to avoid additional score

109

reporting fees. The NCAA Eligibility Center only accepts official test scores sent from the testing agency. Test scores from your high school transcript are not acceptable.

Amateur Status

Student-athletes will be asked a series of questions to determine his or her amateur status when establishing a Certification Account. Generally, more than 90 percent of student-athletes are automatically certified; however, the NCAA Eligibility Center may still require additional information to make an amateur determination. Some activities can impact your amateur status includes:

- Signing a contract with a professional team
- Practicing or playing with a professional team
- Accepting payments, prize money, gifts, or preferential benefits for playing sports
- Agreeing to representation by an agent

High school senior student-athletes, enrolled at a Division I or II college may request an amateurism certification decision from the NCAA Eligibility Center on or after April 1st before fall college enrollment. Students who plan to enroll in college in the spring may request a final amateurism decision on or after October 1st. To request a final amateurism certification, the student-athlete must log in to the Certification Account and request a final amateurism certification determination.

Recruiting

NCAA has strict rules on how and when college representatives contact and recruit high school student-athletes. Athletes should understand the recruiting guidelines to prevent inadvertently breaking the rules. Recruiting occurs when high school student-athletes correspond with college representatives or employees to pursue interests in playing collegiate sports. Recruiting activities might include communicating face-to-face, by telephone, mail, or email or through text messages or social media.

Unofficial and Official College Campus Visits

College-bound student-athletes may visit college campuses for unofficial or official visits. There are guidelines that NCAA requires student-athletes and their parents to follow when considering college tours and visits.

- **Unofficial college visits**: Occur when a student-athlete and his or her parents pay to travel and visit colleges. During an unofficial visit, the only expense the college can only pay for is three tickets to a home sporting event.

- **Official college visits**: Occur when a college pays for a student-athlete and his or her parents to visit a college. The college can pay for (1) transportation to and from the college campus, (2) lodging, (3) three meals per day for the student-athlete and his or her parents, and (4) reasonable entertainment expenses (including three tickets to a home sporting event).

Recruiting Calendars

The NCAA limits recruiting periods throughout the year. Always refer to the NCAA website for rule changes. Table K shows the recruiting periods and what college coaches and representatives can do with student-athletes and their parents. Check the NCAA website for updates on these recruiting periods. A Recruiting Calendar outlines when college-bound student-athletes can be recruited for specific sports.

Table K: Recruiting Periods

Recruiting Periods	College Coaches/Representatives
Contact Period	• May have face-to-face contact with student-athletes or parents • Watch student-athletes practice or compete • Visit student-athletes' high schools • Write or telephone student-athletes or their parents
Evaluation Period	• **May not contact** the student-athletes or parents off the college's campus • Watch student-athletes practice or compete • Visit student-athletes' high schools • Write or telephone student-athletes or their parents
Quiet Period	• **May not have face-to-face contact** with student-athletes or parents off the college's campus • **May not watch** student-athletes practice or compete • **May not visit** the student-athletes' high schools • Write or telephone student-athletes or their parents
Dead Period	• **May not have face-to-face contact** with student-athletes or parents off the college's campus • **May not watch** student-athletes practice or compete • **May not** the student-athletes' high schools • Write or telephone student-athletes or their parents

During the recruiting process, a student-athlete can make a verbal commitment to a college and agree to play sports for a college before he or she signs or is eligible to sign a National Letter of Intent. A student-athlete can make a verbal commitment at any time. The verbal commitment is not binding for the student-athlete or the college.

National Letter of Intent

College-bound student-athletes may sign a National Letter of Intent to attend Division I or II colleges for one academic school year. The National Letter of Intent is a voluntary agreement between the student-athlete and participating NCAA colleges who plan to provide financial aid for one academic year to the student-athlete if the athlete is admitted to the college and has met NCAA eligibility criteria. By signing a National Letter of Intent, the student-athlete official commits to attend a Division I or Division II college for one academic year. The recruiting process ends once a student signs a National Letter of Intent because colleges cannot recruit student-athletes who have already signed a National Letter of Intent.

If a student-athlete decides to attend a different college after signing a National Letter of Intent, he or she may request a release from the contract with the school. If a student-athlete decides not to attend the college where he or she signed the National Letter of Intent but attends a different college, the student-athlete loses a full year of eligibility and must complete a full academic year the new college before regaining eligibility to complete.

NCAA Eligibility for Home School Students

Home School students that wish to play NCAA sports at Division I or II college, should also register with the NCAA Eligibility Center and meet the same requirements as other students. After registering with the NCAA Eligibility Center, visit the NCAA site and review the tool kit designed for home school students at: http://www.ncaa.org/student-athletes/future/home-school-students. NCAA prefers all home school documents to be sent via email by home school administrators or home school umbrella programs. NCAA will not accept documentation submitted by students. Also, NCAA may require home school students to submit additional paperwork such as:

- Acceptable Proof of Graduation: Provide documentation such as a diploma, home school transcript, or state-recognized equivalency exam test result and diploma)
- Signed Statement: describing who manages the home school program (e.g., evaluated coursework, and credits issued) and that home schooling was conducted in accordance with applicable state laws.

- Core-Course Worksheet: For math, English, natural or physical science, social science, foreign language, and other courses.
- Home School Cover Sheet: Submitted with all documentation.

Scholar-Athlete Profile

Athletes should consider developing a *Scholar-Athlete Profile* (**Template 7**) as well. The earlier you develop a *Scholar-Athlete Profile* in high school years, the more time you will have to ensure you are meeting NCAA eligibility requirements and marketing yourself well. This *Scholar-Athlete Profile* can be used to help coaches and other college school officials understand more about you, your academic performance, and athletic performance. Understand that as you develop a *Scholar-Athlete Profile*, you will revise it often. Each time you review your *Scholar-Athlete Profile* you will find that you need to update information because you will new accomplishments, experiences, courses, and activities to include.

Developing and updating your *Scholar-Athlete Profile* will save you tremendous time and energy. To build your Scholar-Athlete Profile, use information from your *Scholar Profile* and incorporate the specific athletic

116

information you may need. Develop a *Scholar Profile* to market yourself and to help others learn more about you in a one-page summary. This document is similar to a resume, but it is different. The *Scholar Profile* seeks to tell the high school story of "you" and highlight your talents and abilities. Depicted in the *Sample Scholar-Athlete Profile* figure is a simple Word document that tells others who you are, what your goals are, and what you have accomplished. Use the *Scholar-Athlete Profile* template provided in this book to tailor it to your interests and experiences.

Sample Scholar-Athlete Profile

SCHOLAR-ATHLETE PROFILE

John Doe
12345 College Bound Drive, City, State Zip Code
Home: (123) 456-789; Mobile: (123) 911-4111
Email: john.doe@yahoo.com
Hudl: http://www.hudl.com/profile/1234531/john.doe
Twitter: @johndoe

NCAA ID: 1234567890
Height: 6'1"   **Weight:** 160 lbs
Football Position(s): FS/SS   **Basketball Position:** Center

Objective: To obtain a four-year degree from an accredited university and to play NCAA sports.

Education: **USA High School**, 1234 High School Lane, City, State 22123
Year: Freshman (Class of 2021); GPA: 3.7

Test Scores: SAT Score (1190); (Reading=670; Math=520)
ACT Composite (21); (English=21; Math=22; Reading=19; Science=21)

High School Staff:
- Football Coach: FirstName LastName, football@highschool.edu, (123) 881-3456
- Basketball Coach: FirstName LastName, basball@highschool.edu, (123) 881-3456
- Counselor: FirstName LastName, counselor@highschool.edu, (123) 881-3457

Employment and Volunteer Experience:
- College Planning Seminar, City, State (2017)
- Church, City, State (2014-2016)
- Club X, Volunteer (2009-2016)

Extracurricular Activities:
- High School, Varsity Football Team, (2017)
- High School, Freshman Boys Basketball Team, (2017-2018)
- Church, Member/Usher, (2008–Present)

Honors and Awards:
- Freshman Basketball Team Most Valuable Player (2018)
- Varsity Football All Conference Honorable Mentions (2017)
- Presidential Academic Excellence Award (2017)

Relevant Courses:
- Geometry
- English 9

At a minimum, a *Scholar-Athlete Profile* should include the following:

- An athletic photo (optional) – Include a professional athletic photo of yourself. If you do not have an athletic photo, take one with a suit on or a simple solid dress or white shirt and tie on. Your photo could help you set a good first impression. Providing a photo is optional. In some cases, photos may be used to discriminate against applicants or candidates. If you have concerns that adding your photo may not be helpful or that it may be used to discriminate against you, do not include one.

- Name, address, email, phone numbers – Provide your contact information. Use your legal name and not a nickname. Also, use an appropriate email address that does not distract from your official business purpose (to get into college or get a scholarship).

- NCAA ID: Include your NCAA ID number. College coaches and officials will want to reference this number to verify your eligibility and to make appropriate contact with you.

- Height and Weight: Include your height (in feet and inches) and your weight (in pounds). Do not exaggerate because you will likely be perceived as dishonest and could lose credibility.

- Sport(s) Played and Position(s): Include the sport(s) and position(s) you played in high school.
- Objective (for college and to play collegiate sports) – Provide a concise statement that tells the reader more about your college and collegiate sports aspirations. Consider sharing what type of college you are interested in, what program or major you wish to study, and other relevant information.
- Educational history (summary) – Specify the high school you attend, the address, your anticipated graduation date, and your GPA.
- Test Scores - Also, specify your SAT/ACT results or the date you plan to take the test.
- High School Staff - Include your high school athletic coach and guidance counselor's name, email and phone number.
- Employment and volunteer history – Specify your job or employment history. College admission professionals like to see if a student is well-rounded and has a work ethic. List your most current job first and list the remaining experiences in descending order, by date. Specify any community service or volunteer work you participated in

since your freshman year. List your most current activity first and list the remaining activities in descending order, by date. College admission professionals like to see students serving their communities.

- Extra-curricular activities – List student organizations and other extra-curricular activities you have taken since your freshman year. Specify if you were a member or if you held a leadership role. List your most current activity first and list the remaining activities in descending order, by date.

- Honors and awards – List your academic, extra-curricular, and athletic honors and awards and specify the year you received them. List your most current honor/award first and list the remaining honors/awards in descending order, by date.

- Relevant Courses – List relevant courses and/or challenging courses (like the NCAA Core 16 courses) you have taken. Do not list every course on your high school transcript.

Scholarships

Student-athletes who plan to attend college and play sports may have opportunities to compete for athletic scholarships. Individual colleges award athletic scholarships.

121

According to the National Collegiate Athletic Association (NCAA), colleges award some form of college athletic scholarships to roughly 2 percent of high school students. Division I and II colleges provide more than $3 billion in scholarships annually to over 150,000 student-athletes. Division III schools do not generally offer scholarship awards to student-athletes, but these students may be eligible for other financial aid, grants, or needs-based scholarships.

SUMMARY

"Life's most persistent and urgent question is, 'What are you doing for others?'" Dr. Martin Luther King, Jr.

As you consider your future aspirations and plans to attend college, think about how you might incorporate the strategies outlined in this book to help achieve your goals. This book highlights specific actions, templates, and resources available to assist along the way. Whether you in middle school or in high school now is the time to start planning. The sooner you begin to plan the more time you will have to be deliberately strategic in your preparation.

There are many aspects to college planning you will have to address, but don't get frustrated. Stay encouraged and do not give up on the process. Remember your end goal to get accepted into college and find adequate funding. Get accepted early and use the rest of your senior year securing all the funding you need. You can do this!

Use the templates provided in this book. Download the templates from my website and customize them as you desire. Also, in the Appendices of this book, there are additional college planning websites and books that you might resourceful. If you find these resources useful or if you have feedback on any of the templates provided, please provide me with your feedback by emailing me at: (author.christiemurray@investnothers.com). Also, share your success stories on my website (https://www.investnothers.com/college-planning) as you get accepted into colleges and are selected for scholarships to encourage others.

While this book is designed to help you get accepted into college, you will then need to focus on how to be successful while matriculating at college. As I tell my sons, don't just Go to college. **Go and Graduate! It's Your Future.** This will require focus, self-discipline, and use effective study skills to achieve the academic success they seek. Chances are, you will discover things you never knew about yourself. Also, when you have an opportunity to help, reach back and pull others forward too! Share this book with others who also could use the help.

THANK YOU!

APPENDIX A: WEBSITE RESOURCES

Now you can find even more specific information about college planning. For example, if you are looking for information on essays, financial aid, scholarships, SAT or ACT testing, college tours, NCAA requirements, and more. These website resources will help you to make better use of your limited time by not having to start from scratch to find valuable information. Note that these links provided in this book may change, break, or get redirected by the website content owners. If the links provided do not work, please use an Internet search engine to find the correct link.

General College Planning Information

- Invest N Others:

  https://www.investnothers.com/college-planning

- College Prep 101:

  http://www.collegeprep101.com/scholarships.html

- Department of Education: *Undergraduate Enrollment in Degree-Granting Postsecondary Institutions*:

  - https://nces.ed.gov/programs/coe/indicator_cha.asp
  - https://nces.ed.gov/fastfacts/display.asp?id=76

College Applications:

- A Complete Guide to the College Application Process: https://www.usnews.com/education/best-colleges/articles/college-application-process
- Common Application: https://www.commonapp.org/
- The Common App: Everything You Need to Know: https://www.usnews.com/education/best-colleges/articles/common-app

College Planning Information

- Cappex College Search: https://www.cappex.com/College and Career Ready: https://www.collegeandcareerready.org
- College Data: https://www.collegedata.com/
- College Ranking: https://www.usnews.com/education
- Education Planner: http://www.educationplanner.org/
- I'm First Plan: http://www.imfirst.org/2012/12/plan/
- Kaplan Factors in College Admission: https://www.kaptest.com/college-prep/applying-to-college/key-factors-in-college-admissions
- Opportunities: Preparing for College: https://ecmc.org/opportunities

- Peterson's Timeline:
  https://www.petersons.com/college-search/planning-list-students-parents.aspx

College Visits and Tours
- 10 Key Places to See on College Tours:
  https://www.usnews.com/education/best-colleges/articles/2018-06-04/10-key-places-to-see-on-college-tours
- eCampus Tours: http://www.ecampustours.com/
- Explore 7 Types of College Campus Visits:
  https://www.usnews.com/education/best-colleges/articles/2017-06-15/explore-7-types-of-college-campus-visits
- US News College Tours:
  https://www.usnews.com/education/best-colleges/right-school/tours

Essay
- 10 Tips to Inspire College Essays:
  https://www.usnews.com/education/best-colleges/slideshows/10-tips-to-inspire-college-essays
- Big Future, Best College Essay:
  https://bigfuture.collegeboard.org/get-in/essays/8-tips-for-crafting-your-best-college-essay

- College Express, College Essay:
  https://www.collegexpress.com/articles-and-advice/admission/articles/college-applications/writing-college-application-essay/
- Common Essay Topics:
  https://www.usnews.com/education/best-colleges/articles/2018-07-09/what-admissions-officers-think-of-3-common-college-essay-topics?int=undefined-rec
- How to Write a College Essay:
  https://www.usnews.com/education/best-colleges/articles/how-to-write-a-college-essay
- Princeton College Essay Advice:
  https://www.princetonreview.com/college-advice/college-essay
- USA News, How to Write a College Essay:
  https://www.usnews.com/education/best-colleges/articles/how-to-write-a-college-essay

Financial Aid

- An Ultimate Guide to Understanding Financial Aid:
  https://www.usnews.com/education/best-colleges/paying-for-college/articles/an-ultimate-guide-

to-understanding-college-financial-aid?int=undefined-rec
- Department of Education - Free Application for Financial Student Aid: https://fafsa.ed.gov
- Sallie Mae: https://www.salliemae.com/research/how-america-pays-for-college/

Homeschooling

- 7 Ways to Think About College When Homeschooling: https://www.straighterline.com/online-education-resources/online-college-for-home-school-2/7-ways-to-think-about-college-when-homeschooling-a-collegebound-high-schooler/
- College Planning Handbook for Homeschooled Students and Families: Regent University: https://www.regent.edu/acad/undergrad/admissions/homeschool/All-In-One-Homeschool-College-Handbook.pdf
- National Home Education Research Institute, Research Facts on Homeschooling: http://www.nheri.org/research/research-facts-on-homeschooling.html
- The Home School Mom: https://www.thehomeschoolmom.com/

- U.S. News and World Report Education: Home-Schooled Teens Ripe for College: http://www.usnews.com/education/high-schools/articles/2012/06/01/home-schooled-teens-ripe-for-college

SAT and ACT Testing

- ACT: https://www.act.org
- ACT Online Prep: https://www.act.org/content/act/en/products-and-services/the-act/test-preparation/act-online-prep.html
- College Board (SAT): https://www.collegeboard.org
- Free Test Prep: http://www.freetestprep.com
- Huntington Test Prep: https://huntingtonhelps.com/test-prep
- Kaplan: https://www.kaptest.com
- Khan Academy: https://www.khanacademy.org
- Kent Prep: https://kentprep.com
- Princeton Review: https://www.princetonreview.com
- Review.com: http://www.reviews.com/act-sat-test-prep-courses/
- Power Score: https://www.powerscore.com/act/courses/

- PrepScholar: https://prepscholar.com/sat/s/
  - Spark Notes: http://www.sparknotes.com/testprep/
  - Study Point: https://www.studypoint.com
- Test-guide: https://www.test-guide.com

Scholarships

- Air Force ROTC: https://www.afrotc.com/scholarships
- Army ROTC: https://www.goarmy.com/rotc/scholarships.html
- Cappex: https://www.cappex.com/
- College Board: www.bigfuture.collegeboard.org
- College Scholarships: www.collegescholarships.com/
- Fastweb: www.fastweb.com
- Naval ROTC: http://www.nrotc.navy.mil/scholarships.html
- Scholly: www.myscholly.com
- Student Scholarships.org: https://studentscholarships.org/#sthash.BzlEVpBW.dpbs
- The Scholarship System: http://thescholarshipsystem.com/home
- Ultimate Guide: How to Find and Secure Scholarships for College: https://www.usnews.com/education/best-

colleges/paying-for-college/articles/how-to-find-and-secure-scholarships-for-college

- Scholarship.com: www.Scholarships.com
- U.S. Department of Labor:
  www.careerinfonet.org/scholarshipsearch

NCAA Eligibility for Student-Athletes

- National Collegiate Athletic Association:
  http://www.ncaa.org/about/student-athlete-eligibility
- NCAA Eligibility Center:
  http://www.ncaa.org/student-athletes/future/eligibility-center
- NCAA Recruiting Calendar:
  http://www.ncaa.org/student-athletes/resources/recruiting-calendars/2017-18-division-i-and-ii-recruiting-calendars

APPENDIX B: BOOK RESOURCES

- "50 Successful Harvard Application Essays: What Worked for Them Can Help You Get into the College of Your Choice" (Harvard)

- "Admission Matters: What Students and Parents Need to Know About Getting into College (Fourth Edition)" (Springer, Sally P. & Reider, Jon)

- "Admission Possible: The "Dare to Be Yourself" Guide for Getting into the Best Colleges for You" (Shevitz, Marjorie Hansen)

- "College Admission: From Application to Acceptance, Step by Step" (Mamlet, Robin & VanDeVelde, Christine)

- "College Planning for Dummies" (Ordovensky, Pat)

- "College Planning for Gifted Students: Choosing and Getting into the Right College" (Berger, Sandra)

- "College Planning for Middle School Students: A Quick Guide" (Wynn, Mychal and Glenn Bascome

- "College Planning: The Ten Biggest Mistakes: And How You Can Avoid Them" (Mastroianni, Michael & Rudderm Rod)

- "Countdown to College: 21 'To Do' Lists for High School" (Pierce, Valerie & Rilly, Cheryl)

- "Fiske Guide to Colleges 2018" (Edward Fiske)
- "Go to College for Free: College Planning ABC's Guide to Finding Scholarships, Financial Aid and Free Tuition Awards for College" (Fabriquer, Manuel & Sterling Publishing Group)
- "Homeschooling High School: Planning Ahead for College Admission (New and Updated)" (Dennis, Jeanne Gowen)
- "How to Be a High School Superstar: A Revolutionary Plan to Get into College by Standing Out (Without Burning Out)" (Newport, Cal)
- "How to Send Your Student to College Without Losing Your Mind or Your Money" (Howard, Shellee)
- "On the Edge: Transitioning Imaginatively to College" (Bierker, Eric & Brown, Jennifer)
- "Paying for College Without Going Broke, 2017 Edition: How to Pay Less for College (College Admissions Guides)" (Princeton Review & Kalman Chany)
- "Teens' Guide to College & Career Planning" (Muchnick, Justin Ross)
- "Teen's Guide to College & Career Planning" (Peterson's)

- "The Christian's Guide to College Admissions" (Durango, Glenda)
- "The Enlightened College Applicant: A New Approach to the Search and Admissions Process" (Belasco, Andrew & Bergman, Dave)
- "The Ultimate College Preparation Blueprint: Everything You Should Expect and Do When Planning for College" (Lewis, Christopher)
- "Waking Up Chase: One Student's Journey to Awakening His Potential" (Bellamy Jr., Darryl)
- "Walking Through the College Planning Process" (Rick Horne)
- "What High Schools Don't Tell You" (Elizabeth Wissner)
- "Where You Go is Not Who You'll Be" (Frant Bruni)

CPSIA information can be obtained
at www.ICGtesting.com
Printed in the USA
FSHW020047240220

9 781977 203212